The
Dynamics of Conflict
Between
Bureaucrats
and
Legislators

Bureaucracies, Public Administration, and Public Policy

Kenneth J. Meier
Series Editor

Bureaucracies, Public Administration,
and Public Policy

The
Dynamics of Conflict
Between
Bureaucrats
and
Legislators

CATHY MARIE JOHNSON

M.E. Sharpe Inc.

Armonk, New York
London, England

Library of Congress Cataloging-in-Publication Data

Johnson, Cathy Marie.
The dynamics of conflict between bureaucrats and legislators /
by Cathy Marie Johnson.
p. cm. — (Bureaucracies, public administration, and public policy)
Includes bibliographical references and index.
ISBN 1-56324-015-7 (cloth)
1. Administrative agencies—United States—Case studies.
2. Bureaucracy—United States—Case studies.
3. Conflict management—United States—Case studies.
4. United States Congress.
5. Policy sciences.
I. Title.
II. Series.
JK585.J65 1992
353.04′0724-dc20
91-28375
CIP

Printed in the United States of America

The paper used in this publication meeets the minimum
requirements of American national standard for information
sciences—permanence of paper for printed library materials,
ANSI Z39.48-1984.

BM   10   9   8   7   6   5   4   3   2   1

To my parents, Patricia and Calvin Johnson

Contents

List of Tables

Foreword

The M.E. Sharpe series on Bureaucracies, Public Policy, and Public Administration is designed as a forum for the best work on bureaucracy and its role in public policy and governance. Although the series is open with regard to approach, methods, and perspectives, especially sought are three related types of research. First, the series hopes to attract theoretically informed, empirical studies of bureaucracy and public administration. Public administration has long been viewed as a theoretical and methodological backwater of political science. This view persists despite a recent accumulation of first-rate research. The series seeks to place public administration at the forefront of empirical analysis within political science. Second, the series is interested in conceptual work that attempts to clarify theoretical issues, set an agenda for research, or provide a focus for professional debates. Third, the series seeks work that challenges the conventional wisdom about how bureaucracies influence public policy or the role of public administration in governance.

The Dynamics of Conflict Between Bureaucracies and Legislators is a challenge to the conventional wisdom about the role of bureaucracy in public policy. We have accepted uncritically the view that public policy in many areas, especially areas of distributive policy, is dominated by policy subsystems. Policy subsystems contain agencies that implement policy, congressional committees that oversee the agencies, and interest groups that benefit from public policy programs. The literature portrays policy subsystems as cooperative; each element of the subsystem can meet its goals by cooperating with other elements in the subsystem. Conflict is avoided because conflict would allow outsiders (other politicians, other interest groups, the president) to intervene in policy affairs and alter the distribution of benefits. Current theories of issue networks and advocacy coalitions attempt to explain what happens when conflict is introduced into a policy subsystem.

Professor Cathy Johnson's study of four agencies—the Bureau of Reclamation, the Bureau of Indian Affairs, the Social and Rehabilitation Service, and the Food and Drug Administration—uses a historical approach to examine conflict and consensus in four policy subsystems. She finds that subsystems are *not* consensual; not only does conflict frequently occur within the policy subsystems, but that conflict is also often resolved within the subsystem without outside intervention.

Professor Johnson's work suggests that several truisms about public policy need to be rethought. First, hitherto policy subsystems have been perceived as major forces supporting the status quo since they deal only with issues that can be resolved to the satisfaction of all subsystem members. While policy subsystems are indeed major forces supporting the status quo, the ability to incorporate conflict and resolve conflict implies that subsystems can produce policy changes without the intervention of other political actors. Professor Johnson's analyses of the Bureau of Reclamation and the Bureau of Indian Affairs reveal major changes in public policy occurring as the result of conflicts in the policy subsystem.

Second, the view that all members of a subsystem benefit from rapid expansion of bureau programs is strongly rejected by the analysis presented. Perhaps no more seductive metaphor in public administration exists than that of a power-hungry bureaucracy bent on program expansion. Such a metaphor, however, is grossly misleading. Conflict occurs over program goals; this study documents several occasions when bureaus resisted program expansion because the expansion required the agency to act contrary to the agency's policy goals. By no means can the agencies examined here be considered imperialist bureaucracies outside the control of other policy-makers. At times the bureaucracy had to be encouraged, prodded, and even threatened to increase its budget and program authority.

Third, the view that conflict is detrimental to public policy is also challenged. Professor Johnson provides evidence that conflict forces policy makers to refine their arguments, gather better information, and seek better policy options. The end result is policy that is more politically feasible, easier to implement, and more likely to have positive benefits.

Professor Johnson's case studies also provide the raw material to address major theoretical questions about bureaucracy and public policy. Two theories guide her work. The self-interest model is based on the premise that all policy actors pursue their own self-interest; bureaus seek larger budgets, interest groups seek more services, legislators seek more votes. Her alternative is the policy model, which holds that these actors have specific policy goals based on their assessments of good public policy. Throughout the analysis, Professor Johnson finds that the self-interest model cannot explain what has occurred but that the policy model does rather well.

Professor Johnson has also provided information that informs a major debate about legislative control of the bureaucracy. Her findings clearly reject the position of the bureau autonomy school that political institutions cannot control the bureaucracy. Her cases reveal a bureaucracy that generally responds to legislative pressure over time. Her findings also challenge the congressional dominance literature that contends bureaucracy is subject to strict control of the legislature. The process has far too much give-and-take and produces results that vary too much to be the result of legislatively imposed controls.

Cathy Johnson has provided us with an excellent illustration of how carefully done case studies can contribute to our theoretical knowledge of bureaucracy and public policy.

Kenneth J. Meier
University of Wisconsin,
Milwaukee

Acknowledgments

Writing a book has differed substantially from any other writing I have done. I would like to thank the Brookings Institution for its financial support. I would also like to thank Joel Aberbach, M. Kent Jennings, John Kingdon, Lawrence Mohr, Mark Peterson, and Kent Weaver for their insightful comments on earlier drafts. Kenneth Meier and Thomas Gais read and reread chapters, making thoughtful comments on every version. Rhonda Danielson, Georgia Duerst-Lahti, Susan Lawrence, and Catherine Novelli provided moral support when my spirits sagged. Last, but of course not least, Hannah Gais stayed close by my side while I put the final touches on this manuscript.

The
Dynamics of Conflict
Between
Bureaucrats
and
Legislators

1

Introduction

"Thrust ivrybody, but cut th' ca-ards."
—Mr. Dooley, *Casual Observations*

Dooley's advice seems appropriate for a government founded on a suspicion of power. As politicians and bureaucrats work with and against each other to advance their respective aims, elements of both cooperation and conflict are likely to emerge. Yet the question of when and why there is conflict between legislators and bureaucrats has largely been ignored. To the extent that any research has been done, it presumes a characterization that is static and undifferentiated. The research tends to draw a picture of an interaction at a particular point, without allowing for variations over time and across issues.

When conflict between legislative committees and executive agencies flares up and *why* it emerges are the central questions of this book. As the role of government has expanded and the bureaucratic state has grown, the relationships between administrative and elected officials have become increasingly important. We can no longer assume that bureaucrats merely implement the policies endorsed by the elected officials; the neat dichotomy between politics and administration cannot reconcile democratic politics with the power of a bureaucracy, or adequately describe a situation where nonelected officials have a significant impact on policy.[1]

Underlying the United States Constitution is a presumption that conflict is desirable because it restrains government and protects the people from tyranny. American government was structured precisely to increase the likelihood of conflict. Politicians selected at different times by different persons would have diverging goals, and the clash of these ambitions would restrain and limit the exercise of power. Institutions with separate and distinct powers would be able to block undesired action because agreement from all branches of government would be needed to advance policies.[2] Even within an institution, conflict was desired. The legislature was divided into two houses so that each chamber would represent different interests. The judicial system was established in the belief that the adversarial process would be most likely to produce truth.[3]

Conflict between bureaucrats and politicians was not built into the constitutional structure of the government. Even so, consensus between these two groups is viewed suspiciously because it implies that opposing viewpoints are not considered and policies are not adjusted to fit additional demands. Consensus emerges not because the relevant participants carefully survey all angles of an issue and reach some agreement, but because contrary views are ignored.[4] Conflict, on the other hand, suggests that opposing interests are not systematically excluded from the decision-making process.

Conflict might enhance the quality of decisions, but we are still somewhat uneasy about clashes between bureaucrats and politicians. Disputes between the president and Congress are legitimate because each has been granted authority by the people. But bureaucrats are not directly responsible to the public; authority is delegated to them by elected officials. Conflict implies that administrators are not complying with the wishes of elected officials. It suggests that bureaucrats are shaping public policy in ways not endorsed by the politicians.

Understanding when and why there is conflict between legislators and bureaucrats will shed light on these questions about the role of the bureaucracy in a democratic state and its effects on policy making. This book examines two different models of legislative-administrative interactions. The hypotheses about conflict and consensus that emerge from these models are tested by analyzing the relationships between four bureaus and their respective authorizing committees from 1961 to 1984. The legislative histories of these agencies were reconstructed by examining an array of public documents and archival material. Interviews with fifty respondents extended and confirmed events reported in the documents.

In the rest of this chapter, I first discuss the approach to understanding relationships between the bureaucracy and Congress that dominates current literature, an approach I have labeled the self-interest model. Then I present an alternative approach—the policy model—and show how it leads to very different hypotheses about the emergence of conflict between executive agencies and legislative committees. Finally I outline my methodology for this study. (See also the Appendix on Research Design at the end of the book.)

Theories of Conflict

The Self-Interest Model

The conventional view of the relationships between Congress and the bureaucracy rests on the assumption that the relevant actors pursue their self-interest. Legislators want to be reelected, bureaucrats want to maximize their budgets, and constituents want to maximize their utility.[5] In order to be reelected, legislators look for programs and projects they can bring their constituents. Bureaucrats endorse these new projects because they allow the agency to grow. Constituents believe they are receiving government benefits yet not paying all of the costs. Because all participants' goals can be met by the same action, expanding an agency's program, consensus between legislators and bureaucrats is the rule rather than the exception.

This consensus between the two groups of decision makers occurs because legislators want to promote the agency's programs. Legislators are attracted to particular committees that address issues important to them and their constituents, and congressional leaders try to satisfy these requests.[6] Because member preferences are given a high priority in the committee assignment process, committees are staffed by legislators who support the programs administered by the agencies they are supposed to oversee. For example, legislators from farming states want to be on the House or Senate Agricultural committees where they can protect the government programs so important to their constituents.[7]

When these legislators look to the bureaucracy, they find administrators sympathetic to their wishes. Like the legislators, the bureaucrats are also advocates for these programs. To enhance their prestige and power, bureaucrats want to maximize their budgets, and expanding their programs is the most direct way to achieve this. In addition, they are pressured by other bureaus in the competition for scarce resources to become advocates, even if they initially believed that the programs they administer should be reduced.[8]

In addition to the consensus that develops because legislators and bureaucrats both want to expand programs, consensus emerges from the indifference of legislators to bureaucratic actions. Legislators with reelection goals pursue activities that require only a superficial examination of administrative actions. They grant authority to the agencies yet have little interest in supervising the daily administration of that authority.

Different authors specify slightly differently the dominant activities of legislators with reelection goals,[9] but they all emphasize the need to focus on issues that create favorable impressions among constituents without also stirring up opposition. David Mayhew, who presents the most comprehensive conception of political activities, argues that legislators in pursuit of reelection devote their time and energy to three activities—advertising, credit claiming, and position taking.[10]

Advertising means ensuring that constituents are not only aware of a legislator but associate him or her with some favorable image. The messages in advertising have little issue content and emphasize style over substance. By credit claiming a legislator promotes the idea that he or she is personally responsible for some desirable government action. The two most common aspects of credit claiming are pork barreling, providing particularized benefits to one's district or state, and casework, assisting a constituent with a specific problem he or she might have with a government program. Finally, the last activity, position taking, covers some of the lawmaking activities that normally one would associate with a legislature. But when engaged in position taking, representatives merely take a stand on an issue; they carefully avoid controversy as well as the detailed consideration so commonly seen as tedious and boring.

A few minutes' reflection on these activities leads quickly to the recognition that they leave little room for serious examination of administrative actions by authorizing committees. Pork barreling indicates a readiness to support the expansion of an agency's program while paying little, and usually only symbolic, attention to the problems of implementation. Position taking and credit claiming involve considerable posturing and symbolic action yet little direct involvement in the administration of policies. Position taking and credit claiming also imply that legislators write vague, general laws,[11] allowing them to avoid conflict and making it appear as though they are tackling the tough, difficult issues, while all along they are leaving the specific decisions to the bureaucracy. Bureaus are given programs to implement yet few detailed instructions on just how they should do that.

Of course, when Congress delegates authority, bureaus make mistakes and constituents complain. Legislators, then, have the opportunity to chide the bureaus and tell them just what they did wrong. But casework rather than oversight is the mechanism most used. Through casework a legislator handles the specific problems or questions of an individual constituent, such as a difficulty with a Social Security check or a complaint about the safety of children's toys. Casework allows a legislator to respond directly to the demands of a constituent, demonstrating his or her concern and responsiveness to the voter's needs. Oversight, a committee investigation into agency actions, provides fewer opportunities to advance legislators' reelection aims because there is no guarantee that constituents will pay any attention to the proceedings.[12] When it does occur, it is often political and symbolic, allowing the legislators to present a picture of dedicated, hard-working representatives protecting the public interest while still avoiding the nitty-gritty, often conflictual, and sometimes boring issues involved in the administration of the laws.

This view of interactions between legislators and administrators has been refined through analysis of subgovernments, the dominant way in which political scientists model the making of public policy in the United States.[13] A number of case studies have documented the importance of subgovernments—often called "iron triangles"—in a variety of policy areas, including agriculture, energy, water policy, and even social welfare programs.[14] Consisting of a congressional committee, an agency, and an interest group, a subgovernment is an autonomous unit that makes the policy decisions in a particular issue area. Because the various decision makers have similar interests, policy making tends to be consensual; differences are minor and resolved through negotiations. If conflict occurs, it is because the issue is no longer controlled by the subgovernment but is addressed by the president, congressional leaders, and political parties on the House and Senate floor.[15]

Building on Theodore Lowi's work,[16] Randall Ripley and Grace Franklin have developed hypotheses about when subgovernments are influential in policy making.[17] Subgovernments dominate in distributive policies, policies subsidizing private activities that are supposed to be desirable to the entire society.[18] For example, the government shores up agriculture through price supports and aids new businesses with grants and loans. Because the policies provide tangible and easily disaggregated benefits to the individuals, groups, or corporations engaging in these activities, the program beneficiaries are likely to be well organized and politically active. However, those paying the costs of the programs are unlikely to be organized, partly because the costs are not obvious—after all, these are programs that are supposed to be good for the entire society—and partly because the costs are dispersed across the nation, making collective action difficult to achieve.[19] Consensus arises because opposing viewpoints are not represented in the political process and thus cannot break up the "cozy triangle" of a congressional committee,[20] an agency, and an interest group all promoting policies in their self-interest.

In redistributive and regulatory policy areas, subgovernments lose influence to the president, congressional leaders, and political parties. Regulatory policy is designed to protect the public by specifying the conditions under which certain actions can be taken by the private sector.[21] For example, government policies specify that employers have to protect workers, businesses have to minimize air and water pollution, and pharmaceutical companies have to show that their prescription drugs are both safe and effective before they can be marketed. Because regulatory policies involve setting a general rule of law, the issues are not easily disaggregated. The subgovernments, so accomplished at making disaggregative policies, lose authority to the full House and Senate, settings where general rules can be hammered out by political parties and congressional leaders.

Like regulatory policy, redistributive policy also involves the establishment of principles and general rules. Redistributive issues are framed in ideological terms because the policies involve the allocation of values among clearly identified winners and losers.[22] For example, War on Poverty programs such as Job Corps and Legal Services raise questions about the role of the federal government. In redistributive policies, coalitions form and reform, presidents target the issues as a principal part of their domestic agenda, Democrats and Republicans adopt clear and differing stands on the issues. The bipartisan, consensual subgovernments are abandoned; the issues are battled out on the floor of Congress with the full participation of the president and the political parties.

This typology of policies and the subsequent politics predicts that because bureaus administering regulatory and redistributive policies are unlikely to operate in subgovernments, they face a more conflictual environment. As additional actors such as the president and the political parties enter the fray, the heightened salience and the greater participation result in more conflict in these policy areas. However, this account is less than complete. The conflict is among a variety of decision makers, not necessarily the agencies and their authorizing committees. The approach tells us little about the relationships between the bureaus and their committees, working groups that set the groundwork for the legislative discussions on the floor. The responses of the agencies and thus their interactions with congressional committees in redistributive and regulatory policy are not clear. If the president and the Congress square off, does the agency follow the lead of its chief executive officer and side with the president in the dispute? In an issue characterized by partisan conflict with the majority party dominating the minority party, does the agency accede to the majority position even if it believes it is poor public policy? The subgovernment analysis provides little insight into the relationships between agencies and committees beyond the distributive policy area.

Studies of subgovernments are usually cross-sectional, taking a snapshot of a political relationship at a particular point in time. Scholars have developed expectations of what happens over time by relying on a number of cross-sectional studies.[23] The dominant expectation is that conflictual issues are raised by individuals outside of the subgovernment. Subgovernment participants, so accustomed to defining issues in well-established ways, either do not anticipate these other concerns or they refuse to consider them. Thus, the issues can only be raised when new interests enter from the outside and push their concerns onto the agenda. For example, in 1974 the sugar subgovernment collapsed after consumer groups raised a new issue—protecting consumers from high prices—in a policy arena defined by concern over subsidies to one sector of agriculture.[24]

These conflictual issues are not only raised by outsiders; they are also disruptive. Because a dispute centers on the fundamental issue of the policy area, conflict spills over into a broad array of matters that a committee and agency have to decide. When conflict occurs, it characterizes the entire set of interactions between the agency and the committees. The system is tightly coupled; conflict over one issue cannot be separated from another issue.

This conception of conflict is very clear in descriptions of subgovernment relationships. One should also note that this conception follows logically from assumptions of the self-interest model. Both the self-interest model and the subgovernment variant assume that the critical elements affecting the relations between a bureau and its committee are the type of policy the agency administers and the constitutional structure of political institutions. Because these are highly aggregated forces that tend to be constant within an agency's jurisdiction and across time, conflict means that there has been a fundamental and enduring shift in the agency–committee interactions. Conflict, then, upsets the standard practice of making decisions, altering the pattern of interactions among decision makers.[25] The subgovernment cannot manage or contain the conflict. When confronted by these external threats, it is forced either to adapt or to disintegrate. A subgovernment can adapt by conceding not to pursue its earlier policy. It will disintegrate if it allows the issue to be resolved through some other decision-making mechanism.

This perspective is buttressed by research arguing that subgovernments have weakened, giving rise to issue networks and group conflict. Hugh Heclo coined the term *issue networks*, arguing that a broad variety of interests lobbied for change in a given policy area.[26] What these issue networks meant in terms of conflict was not entirely clear to Heclo. Obviously, the consensus of the iron triangles had given way, but that weakening did not automatically mean conflict would result because policy activists shared a core set of views that would frame their interactions. Thomas Gais, Mark Peterson, and Jack Walker are more adamant in arguing that conflict arises with the weakening of subgovernments.[27] Relying on their survey of interest groups, Gais et al. argue that the iron triangles of the 1940s and 1950s have weakened, and that one of the major reasons is the "rise to prominence of contentious new interest groups" organized around ideological causes.[28] Group conflict is the result as these new groups raise different perspectives on the issues and engage in confrontational outside strategies.

Daniel McCool argues that subgovernments remain strong,[29] despite the changes in policy making outlined by various scholars.[30] According to McCool, subgovernments have adapted to new interests by fragmenting power and accommodating different views. Additional subgovernments centered around the new interests were created, and the old subgovernments ceded some of their decision-making authority to the new subgovernments. Thus, distributive policy and the pattern of politics that produces it remain prevalent in Congress.[31]

Many scholars have complained that the subgovernment model is conceptually fuzzy. Others have argued that it does not describe accurately policy making in the 1980s. Despite these criticisms, support for an alternative model of policy making has not emerged. The subgovernment model remains dominant in writing about American politics, and its connection to the simpler self-interest model has not been severed.

The self-interest model and the subgovernment variant lead to a clear set of hypotheses about the extent of consensus and the emergence of conflict between agencies and committees. First, consensus between legislators and bureaucrats will be the norm, not the exception. Second, authorizing committees will pay relatively little attention to the way in which agencies administer programs. Oversight will be infrequent. When it occurs, it will be in response to a crisis and will involve a rather superficial examination of agency behavior. Third, when conflict arises, it will be raised by forces outside of the subgovernment. Fourth, conflict will focus on the fundamental issue of the policy area and will disrupt the standard practices of decision making. Fifth, consensus will be more prevalent in distributive policy areas than in regulatory or redistributive policies. Last, relationships between agencies and committees in regulatory and redistributive policies are unclear.

The Policy Model

As will be demonstrated throughout this book, the types of conflicts and the pattern of disputes between agencies and committees do not fit the hypotheses of the self-interest model. Conflict between the agencies and their committees occurs frequently, and much of the conflict is generated by the authorizing committees themselves as they try to ensure that administrative practices are consistent with their policy views. Conflict does not disrupt standard decision-making practices because a dispute on one issue, even a fundamental overarching question, does not dictate what happens on other issues. In addition, the typology of policies in subgovernment analysis is not helpful in understanding when and why the four agencies clash with their committees.

As an alternative to the self-interest model, this book develops a different picture of legislators and bureaucrats, one that accounts for more conflict between them and greater variation in their relationships over time. In the policy model both legislators and bureaucrats have policy goals, and the pursuit of these goals shapes their interactions. Agencies have missions that direct their actions and programs they want to accomplish. Legislators try to ensure that bureaucratic policies and administrative practices are consistent with the wishes of the legislature.

Although the policy model focuses on the same individuals as the self-interest model, it makes very different assumptions about the motivations of bureaucrats and legislators. The motivations that form the basis of the self-interest model are not irrelevant in the policy model, but they are clearly secondary. Legislators want to be reelected, but it is their policy views, not their reelection goals, that shape an authorizing committee's interactions with the bureaucracy. Similarly, bureaus will push for budgetary growth, but this goal is clearly subordinate to their policy interests.

Like the self-interest model, the policy model focuses on those legislators who sit on particular committees. However, the policy model emphasizes their expertise and interest in promoting their policy stances, not their concern with reelection. Committees are staffed by individuals who build expertise in a policy area because they have a strong interest in the issues addressed by the specific committees. Even within a committee, members specialize; a few individuals will decide to make a particular policy their area of expertise. These legislators build up seniority on the committees and over time become the chairs and ranking minority members of subcommittees and full committees. Their positions allow them to set the agendas of their respective organizations.

These legislators, called preference outliers by Kenneth Shepsle and Barry Weingast,[32] have many reasons to monitor bureaucratic actions and exert independence in policy making. They are more likely than the average legislator to focus on the details of legislation, implementation, and agency management practices. First, some legislators act as entrepreneurs; they seek out innovative legislative proposals that will put their names in history books, further an ideological cause, or establish a record for higher office.[33] Senator Edmund Muskie (D–ME), when launching a bid for the presidency, aggressively pursued clean air and water legislation.[34] Representative Richard Gephardt (D–MO), as a junior member on the House Ways and Means Committee, picked out tax reform as an issue to establish a name. Senator Jesse Helms (R–NC) used his position as ranking minority member of the Senate Foreign Relations Committee to promote an array of conservative causes, especially his animosity toward communism.[35]

Second, legislative action is one way to respond to electoral trends, to show constituents that their concerns have been heard and acted upon. Elections give politicians a sense of what the electorate is thinking and what issues seem to be important.[36] Election outcomes also apprise an individual of his or her standing with the constituency. After an uncomfortably close reelection race, Senator Warren Magnuson (D–WA) picked out consumer safety as a legislative cause to bolster his sagging political career. As chair of the Commerce Committee he pushed legislation dealing with meat and fish inspections and the safety of diet pills, toys, and fabrics.[37]

Third, some legislators want to be known as experts on a particular issue. Keeping a watchful eye on a particular agency's programs is one way to establish as well as maintain that specialization.[38] Sam Nunn (D–GA) earned a reputation as a "500-pound gorilla" on defense issues through rigorous and unstinting attention to defense policy. As chair of the Senate Armed Services Committee, he kept careful tabs on defense spending, pushing for a more efficient and balanced approach to defense.[39]

The self-interest model disparages the importance of such oversight activities because they do not attract much visibility for legislators seeking reelection. One should bear in mind, however, that although oversight may not have high visibility, it also has few costs, making it an attractive strategy for legislative experts. The most significant cost is the opportunity cost, the time devoted to oversight that could have been spent on some other activity. No other costs are associated with oversight. If the oversight is effective, legislators can claim credit. If it fails to change administrative behavior, they can always blame the bureaucracy, charging that it is bound by inertia, captured by special interests, or flagrantly abusing legislative authority. Regardless of the outcome, legislators can build up their reputations as specialists.

Finally, legislators want to exert control over the bureaucracy in order to protect the power of their institution. One cannot deny that members are concerned about the power of Congress and that they will adopt institutional practices and policies in order to bolster and protect it. Reforms of the 1970s, such as the War Powers Act and the Budget and Impoundment Control Act, were designed to enhance the power of Congress vis-à-vis the president.[40] But it is not only the president that Congress worries about. Bureaucrats running rampant over legislative wishes arouse concern that Congress as an institution is being weakened by the bureaucrats' abuse of power. Legislators develop devices, such as the legislative veto, to ensure the primacy of congressional views. In fact, Congress continued to pass legislation with veto provisions, even after the Supreme Court declared the device unconstitutional.[41]

Thus, legislators have a variety of incentives—personal, ideological, and institutional—to fashion laws and regulations that meet their own policy preferences rather than those of the bureaucracy. Even when they support the programs administered by a bureau, they want those programs to fit with their own conception of what needs to be done. They will use their formal positions as chairs and ranking minority members of subcommittees and full committees to advance their notion of good public policy.

One could question why an agency would not simply follow the policy guidelines advanced by the committees and thus avoid any problems created by clashing with Congress. Such a strategy is particularly difficult for an agency to pursue. Even if an agency wanted to follow the legislature, it would be impossible to do so in many cases. Agencies usually deal with more than one committee. If the committees disagree, the path the agency should follow is unclear. Guidelines by appropriations committees often contradict those of the authorizing committees. Committees change their positions over time as they respond to the new demands of constituents and legislators.[42] Because of discord, a committee may choose not to act on a particular issue; the agency does not always have a similar luxury. Often it must make some decision on the matter in order to deal with pressing business.

More important, agencies will not always comply with congressional wishes because they develop their own policy perspectives. Like legislators, administrators use their positions to promote these policies. The policy goals of a committee and an agency will often diverge because some forces influence the bureau yet not the committee. To adhere to legislative will, the agency would have to subordinate its policy goals to those of the committee. Despite good intentions, congressional views will not dominate automatically.

Just as legislators have reasons to shape policy to meet their own perspectives, agencies pursue policy goals.[43] They use these goals as benchmarks to evaluate prospective programs and actions. Initially, the policy goals of a new agency are congruent with the goals of the political coalition that ruled when the agency was established.[44] Over time, however, the perspectives of committees and agencies diverge as these decision makers are affected differently by different events such as election outcomes, personnel changes, and program implementation.

An authorizing committee is only one of several forces in an agency's environment that influences its policies. A bureau has to pay attention to the demands and guidelines of other institutions such as the courts, the president, and interest groups. Judicial interpretation of congressional statutes often means that agencies are required to pursue certain activities that Congress has not specifically required. The Environmental Protection Agency was forced by the courts to develop a program to prevent the deterioration of air quality in areas with air much cleaner than the national standards, despite congressional inattention to this issue.[45] Philip Selznick's classic study of the Tennessee Valley Authority shows how an agency was forced to adapt its policies to meet demands of clientele groups.[46] President Reagan altered the policies of many regulatory agencies when he recruited political appointees adamant about reducing government interference with business.[47]

In addition, agency views will be shaped by internal forces such as personnel changes, professional knowledge, and program implementation. When agencies recruit personnel with different backgrounds, approaches to issues can shift dramatically. In the 1950s the Department of Justice changed its recruitment practices and began searching nationwide to hire the top law school graduates. The Antitrust Division's approach to cases was altered when these young aggressive lawyers pushed for trial experience in order to advance their careers.[48] Several administrators in the Bureau of Reclamation clung tightly to the mission of providing water for the West. Because they had grown up during the dust bowl days, they knew that water was not a resource one could take for granted.[49]

New perspectives in the professions relevant to agency programs also affect policy views. Advancements in academic disciplines such as biochemistry, economics, and child development alter the ways in which agencies define problems, their assumptions about human behavior, and the solutions available to the agency. For example, changes in economists' understanding of markets and antitrust practices in the 1970s led to different enforcement policies by the Antitrust Division of the Department of Justice in the 1980s.[50]

Experience also shapes an agency's view of what policies are necessary as well as feasible. Agencies develop expertise as they administer programs. Agencies have to figure out how to set up the procedures to implement new programs. In turn these standard operating procedures provide the feedback to evaluate the program, allowing agencies to learn from the failures and successes of past policies.[51] Feedback also comes from program opponents, who argue that the agency has not focused on the true problem, does not understand the cause of the problem, and has adopted the wrong solution to the problem. Agencies adjust their approaches as they recognize and accommodate these opponents.[52] Thus, over time an agency will form its own conceptions of what a policy should be.

Agencies with policy goals behave in identifiable ways, and this behavior differs from that of the budget-maximizing bureaus in the self-interest model. First, agencies with policy goals do not operate in a vacuum, nor do goals shift with the wind. Agency behavior is framed by its historical context. Much like individuals, agencies carry the baggage of their past. Past events are constraints that shape agency perspectives, choices, and reactions to external demands. The interests of clientele groups sway reactions to new policies and programs.[53] Decisions about the direction of an agency's program restrain responses to future programs.[54] Earlier choices do not necessarily dictate current decisions, but they establish boundaries and guidelines that constrain these decisions.

Second, the pursuit of policy goals implies that bureaucrats act as advocates for those policies they hold dear, but it does not imply that they will always seek expansion of their tasks and programs. They will seek additional resources to carry out their tasks, and they will defend the legitimacy of their policies from those who question them. New tasks and programs will be evaluated according to how they "fit" with existing policy goals. Bureaucrats will also oppose new programs that they believe would conflict with or jeopardize existing responsibilities.[55] If an agency's mission is defined by the clientele that it serves, new policies that jeopardize current constituents will not be endorsed.

Although it is commonly believed that agencies seek to expand, there are many examples to the contrary. Agencies have often opposed the adoption of new tasks. As the head of the Federal Bureau of Investigation, J. Edgar Hoover resisted new responsibilities that would have altered the central tasks of agents.[56] After a reorganization within the Department of Health, Education, and Welfare in 1967, the Children's Bureau acquired the responsibility for providing services to children receiving Aid to Families with Dependent Children, a responsibility it did not really want. The new task clashed with the policies the Children's Bureau originally pursued and required a change in the agency's mission and operations.[57] In 1988 the Pentagon opposed an expanded role for the military in enforcement of drug laws, claiming that the duties would jeopardize its mission of national security.[58]

These are clear examples of agencies resisting programmatic change because of the way in which they defined their policy goals. The bureaucracy's unwillingness to adopt programs that do not mesh with existing tasks is responsible for the more general, and more common, criticisms of bureaucratic rigidity, inertia, and conservatism. Presidents create new agencies to administer new programs because they fear that existing bureaus will not endorse the new policy.[59] Anthony Downs argues that agencies "rigidify" or "ossify" as they grow old.[60] Bruce Heady concludes that innovation and radical change are rarely found in bureaucrats' legislative proposals because "officials normally frame policy programs which fit within the context of the existing objectives pursued by their department."[61]

Third, as an agency develops expertise and familiarity with program implementation, it develops its own views of what will work and what will not. In order to protect the integrity of these policy views, bureaucrats will oppose programs that they believe cannot be executed. Bureaucrats do not want legislators to set up unrealistic expectations and then criticize the agency for not achieving them. They do not want the legislature to have the opportunity to make their policy approaches look ridiculous. This protective action by bureaucrats could lead to conflict with congressional committees in the short run as bureaucrats are willing to risk some conflict now in order to avoid blame and criticism later. They will avoid policies that could jeopardize the good standing of the agency in the future.

Finally, to give it room to pursue its policy goals, an agency wants discretion. Discretion allows the agency to clear up discrepancies in the law, determine what procedures should be used to implement a program, and fit new procedures in with old. Congress recognizes that some discretion is necessary to administer any program, but it also realizes that too much discretion gives the bureaucracy leeway to ignore legislative wishes. For example, pro-life representatives disliked provisions allowing Medicaid funding for abortion when it was "medically necessary" because they felt that HEW regulations would be too lax, rendering the restrictive appropriations rider meaningless.[62]

Even though the agency desires discretion, it recognizes that politicians have important policy-making roles. The agency cannot act entirely on its own; politicians must legitimize some of its plans through legislation. For example, after a loophole was discovered in federal banking law, the Federal Reserve Board placed a moratorium on granting charters to nonbanks. Even though the Fed could have closed the loophole administratively, it set up the moratorium to give Congress the time to act on the issue.[63] Bureaucrats look to legislators to establish overarching principles and missions, to decide what major goals the agency should be addressing. Politicians provide the energy; bureaucrats find the equilibrium.[64]

Like the self-interest model, the policy model's assumptions yield a clear set of hypotheses about the extent and emergence of conflict. But the hypotheses of the policy model provide a contrasting view of the nature and extent of conflict as well as of the types of disputes that arise. All together, these hypotheses draw a very different picture of the relationships between an agency and its authorizing committees than the self-interest model.

First, there is no reason to assume that conflict is rare; to the contrary, conflict is inevitable. In the policy model conflict arises as legislators and bureaus push for the dominance of their own policy views. In the self-interest model, consensus arises because one policy—expanding an agency's program—satisfies the demands of all participants. But in the policy model no one solution will satisfy everyone automatically; the policy goals of the agency and the committee diverge as they are affected differently by different events.

Second, conflict will be raised by insiders as well as outsiders. The closed subgovernment of the self-interest model is replaced by one that is open to a variety of perspectives. Legislators on the authorizing committees, the preference outliers, play a key role in opening up these debates. Because they have so many reasons to be engrossed in the policy issues and to watch the bureaucracy, they will be especially attuned to a variety of issues. They will not delimit the deliberations between the agency and the committee by ignoring possibly conflictual issues.

Third, when conflict arises, it will not disrupt the standard decision-making procedures of the agency and committee. When faced with conflict, a subgovernment will not have to adapt or disintegrate because conflict on one issue, even a fundamental question of the policy area, will not set the tone for all other interactions. Nor will conflict at one time necessarily lead to conflict at a later time. The subgovernment will manage the conflict in the sense that it will prevent it from affecting all other issues. It will discover ways to make decisions even when facing conflict on an overarching policy issue. The system will be loosely coupled, rather than tightly knit as in the self-interest model.[65]

Fourth, across agencies there will be more similarities in relationships with committees in the policy model than in the self-interest model. In the policy model the type of policy an agency administers does not determine the politics. Contrary to the self-interest model, it does not predict that distributive policies operate in consensual subgovernments, and regulatory and redistributive policies encounter considerable conflict because they are addressed on the House and Senate floor.

In addition to these four hypotheses about the extent and nature of conflict, the policy model yields hypotheses about the kinds of disputes that are likely to arise. These hypotheses center around the scope of an agency's authority as well as the way that authority is exercised once it has been granted to a bureau. In the self-interest model the scope of the agency's authority is not an unsettling question because both the legislators and the administrators want the programs to grow. The policy model, however, provides for the possibility of considerable conflict about the scope of an agency's authority, even for well-established bureaus. Questions about scope will appear frequently on a committee's agenda as legislators with policy goals maintain a strong interest in the programs and goals of an agency. Because agencies evaluate these issues according to their policy goals, their responses to proposals to add new tasks or limit their scope are not as predictable as those of the budget-maximizing bureaus.

First, the policy model predicts that conflict will arise when bureaucrats do not support additional tasks and responsibilities. In the self-interest model such a scenario is unthinkable. Budget-maximizing bureaus would always support additional responsibilities because they could be used to press for additional appropriations.[66] But as was discussed earlier, bureaucrats with policy goals have a number of reasons to oppose additional responsibilities. Bureaucrats will oppose new tasks that conflict with the interests of their traditional clientele. New tasks that do not fit easily with existing goals will be viewed with much skepticism. Legislators who want to add tasks that do not fit with the agency's current mission will frequently be frustrated by the bureau's response.

Bureaucrats will oppose another type of new task, and that is one that they feel jeopardizes the integrity of their agency. Bureaucrats have no reason to support new tasks that they feel are impossible to do. This reaction will be more prevalent when agencies are frequently criticized about the way in which they administer the laws. Bureaucrats are probably aware that politicians overestimate the changes that can be accomplished by legislative programs, so they would tone down the rhetoric in the legislative debate. But even after this adjustment, bureaucrats would view some proposals as merely unmanageable. They have every reason to oppose these, especially if they believe that they will later be criticized for what they could not possibly have accomplished.

Second, in the policy model conflict will not be inevitable if the legislature moves to limit the scope of the agency. The budget-maximizing bureaus of the self-interest model would always oppose any reductions in their programmatic responsibilities because they would lead to diminished opportunities for growth if not outright budget cuts. As long as subgovernments control the decision making, such a proposal is highly unlikely. However, it could be generated if outsiders had the opportunity to register their opposition. In such a scenario conflict would arise as the bureaus tried to prevent the cuts.

Almost every assumption about the goals of bureaucratic behavior implies that a bureau will resist cuts in its budget and reductions in its authority. The goals of maximizing a budget, providing budget security, and minimizing uncertainty all suggest that a bureau would oppose reductions in its budget. A policy goal provides a similar expectation. If the agency believed in its mission, it would not acquiesce to the legislature's aim of restricting the program. Conflict between an agency and its congressional committees will develop when committees press for reduced authority and budget outlays.

What is different about the policy model, however, is that it allows for the possibility that bureaucrats would approve of changes that might reduce the size or responsibilities of the agency if such limitations would help them meet policy goals. Thus, conflict will not always develop when the legislature supports policies that limit the scope of the agency. This situation will not occur frequently because it requires that bureaucrats repudiate, at least to some extent, their past efforts. It will be most likely to occur when agency officials become dissatisfied with old approaches and start searching for new direction. Political appointees or civil servants new to the agency would be the forces behind these changes because long-time workers would be more likely to believe that their previous actions promoted policy achievements.[67]

In the policy model disputes do not center only around the scope of an agency's authority; they also arise over questions about the way the authority is exercised. Legislators with a strong interest in a particular agency's program will decide to watch the agency's actions closely. Policy decisions may be investigated by a committee to determine if the agency made the correct decision. Committee members may become disgruntled with an agency's policies and tighten controls through legislative changes. Authorization for new programs may include very detailed procedures that an agency must follow when implementing the program.

Legislative proposals to reduce an agency's discretion will not be warmly received by an agency. Because the agency wants discretion in order to advance its policy views, it will resent the congressional interference into what it sees as day-to-day administrative decisions. An agency will oppose committee proposals that specify in great detail the actions the agency has to take when implementing the program. Consensus on broad general bills that leave the details of the implementation to the agency will be more likely.

Conflicts over which group of decision makers should determine the nitty-gritty details will carry over into oversight. Committees investigating bureaucratic procedures will encounter some opposition, especially if the legislators believe that they have a better grasp of what should be done than the agency. Because they believe they have the expertise to make decisions, agency officials will resent second-guessing of their decisions by legislators. They will defend the procedures they have used to administer programs.

These two models, the policy model and the self-interest model, rest on different assumptions about the goals of both legislators and bureaucrats. As a result, they lead to different hypotheses about the nature and extent of conflict as well as the actions that lead to it. In the self-interest model, consensus is the norm, and conflict is rare. Consensus arises because subgovernments include those actors with similar views and exclude the opposition. Conflict develops when this opposition breaks open the subgovernment, forcing the issue to be debated in a larger framework, one that allows alternative views to be aired. Thus, conflict is disruptive; it fractures the subgovernment and permanently alters standard decision-making patterns.

In the policy model, conflict is unavoidable as both legislators and bureaucrats push forward with policy goals which inevitably diverge. Legislators have a keen interest in assuring that bureaus comply with their directives. Bureaucrats hope to gain the discretion they need to advance the actions they believe are necessary and feasible. Because subgovernments are not closed, new issues and different perspectives can be heard. As bureaus and committees interact, disputes emerge and are resolved. Because conflict on one issue does not frame interactions on all other issues, it is manageable and does not shatter the subgovernment.

Methodology

The Problem of Group Goals

This theoretical framework uses the concept of a group goal, the idea that people within a bureau or a committee share a common goal. I refer to an agency or a committee as though it is a unified, individualized entity, much as law refers to a corporation as an individual. Certainly, this is somewhat unrealistic. Much research, particularly on organizations, outlines the difficulties with such an approach.[68] In the most comprehensive analysis, Richard Cyert and James March argue that goals are created out of the bargaining among individuals, an organization can have many goals, and goals shift over time.[69]

For the purposes of this research, however, a group goal is a useful and necessary simplifying assumption. It is also not totally unreasonable. An agency can develop and maintain an ideology through the recruitment and socialization of new civil servants. Individuals who agree with the objectives of the agency may be more likely to be hired. If recruits' perspectives were inconsistent with the ideology of the agency, they could be socialized, encouraged to conform, or fired. Research on both the Forest Service and the Foreign Service concludes that these agencies developed a notion of an elite corps and socialized their new recruits to accept that idea.[70] Also, divisions within an agency may have different goals, but they will not necessarily conflict. For example, the Food and Drug divisions of the Food and Drug Administration may well have different goals, but the actions of one unit do not affect the actions of another because the tasks are not related. The agency has to determine its priorities for resources, but it does not have to reconcile conflicting behaviors. Work on congressional committees suggests that committee members tend to have very similar goals, allowing one to aggregate these individual goals to a committee goal.[71] In addition, my research relies on formal congressional behavior, so minority views are subordinated to majority decisions.

Most of the time the assumption of a group goal does not present problems in the study of these four agencies. Even so, differences among bureaucrats and committee members are not difficult to imagine. A common split is between political appointees and career civil servants; the central office of an agency may not agree with its field offices; and majority and minority party members on a committee may have very different views of the problems and the solutions. Disparate views are sometimes important, especially in the policy model. Divisions within committees or within bureaus help the airing of various issue positions. When the divisions affect a decision, the assumption of the group goal is dropped, and the various factions are discussed.

Definition and Indicators of Conflict

Conflict is defined as disagreement between the committee and the bureau over policies and administrative procedures when that disagreement is expressed by formal action. I do not deal with those instances in which a member is annoyed with the agency yet does not act on that disapproval, because these situations have little effect on the legislature's and the bureau's policy decisions. When such disagreement is found, it is included in the analysis if it leads to formal committee action or if it is an example of general committee dissatisfaction.

Indicators of conflict are:

1. Differences in positions on bills. Minor disagreement in the context of overall agreement on a bill is considered to be approval.
2. Committee refusal to act on an issue when the agency desires such action.
3. Congressional proceedings to prevent or require a specific agency action that the agency has the legal authority to take.
4. Congressional investigation of an agency's administration of the law even if the agency agrees with the criticism. The agency's acceptance of the criticism indicates either a strategy to reduce conflict or the success of the congressional oversight rather than initial consensus. I refer to this as congressional oversight.[72]

Throughout the analysis, I discriminate between conflict over management or administrative practices and conflict over policy. Although I do not intend to resurrect the policy–administration dichotomy, I do distinguish between those cases when the law as written is not disputed but the law as implemented by the agency is a matter of concern and those cases in which there is disagreement over how the law should be written. For example, in the dispute over the regulation of medical devices, Congress believed the law was fine. The problem was the Food and Drug Administration's (FDA) implementation of the law. At other times, congressional committees and the FDA disagreed about the structure of the law.

In analyzing these relationships, one central problem is symbolic action.[73] A committee may criticize an agency with little concern that the disliked action be changed. A member may introduce a bill with no intention of seeing that bill adopted. What may appear to be conflict between the agency and the committee may be purely ceremonial, with little concern behind the facade.

Symbolic action, however, is not without its consequences. Members of Congress may conduct oversight hearings merely to gain publicity or show the voters back home that they are doing something about the problems in the government with little concern about really effecting change. For the agency, though, these hearings are not inconsequential. Bad press is generated; constituents become upset about the agency's ineptness; other members of Congress lose faith in the agency's abilities to administer programs. For the members of the committee, the conflict may be a sham. For the agency, the conflict may have much more long-lasting and substantial effects.

Selection of the Agencies

The four agencies selected for analysis are the Bureau of Indian Affairs and the Bureau of Reclamation, both in the Department of Interior, and the Food and Drug Administration (FDA) and the Social and Rehabilitation Service in the former Department of Health, Education, and Welfare. I selected these four agencies because they varied along a crucial theoretical dimension—the typology of subgovernment analysis. I wanted to study conflict in a diverse set of agencies to enhance the possibility of generalizing from the findings.

The Bureau of Reclamation administers classic distributive policy. The bureau's central mission is to construct water projects that irrigate and reclaim land in seventeen western states. It provides benefits to a concentrated and well-organized group, and costs are dispersed across the country. The recent organization of environmental groups allows me to examine the hypotheses about the permeability of subgovernments.

The Bureau of Indian Affairs is difficult to place in the policy typology because of the diverse nature of its responsibilities. But because it provides concentrated benefits to an easily identified and concentrated clientele, it fits the notion of distributive policy. However, it provides a nice contrast to the Bureau of Reclamation because its clientele has few resources and because the opposition is often organized and vociferous.

The Food and Drug Administration implements regulatory policy, protecting consumers from unsafe foods, drugs, and cosmetics. The agency often finds itself caught between the conflicting demands of consumer groups and the food and drug industries. Cries that the Food and Drug Administration is captured by the industries it regulates are often heard, but the agency also has to respond to legislative and interest-group demands to protect consumers. The FDA seems to encounter a more diverse, and more divisive, political environment than the other agencies.[74]

The Social and Rehabilitation Service administered redistributive policy. Created in 1967 and disbanded in 1977, the service was supposed to consolidate many of the public assistance programs, such as Medicaid, social services, and vocational rehabilitation. Unlike the other three agencies, the agency was never firmly entrenched; questions of the juxtaposition of the programs it administered plagued the agency during its entire existence.

In the next four chapters I discuss the relationships between each agency and its congressional committees, outlining the nuances in these interactions as conflict rises and falls. In the last chapter I consider the relationships across the agencies, reflecting on the validity of the two models. These chapters demonstrate that the policy model provides a much more thorough and enlightened explanation of these interactions than the self-interest model. Policy does not determine the politics. Although these four agencies are very different in the types of programs they administer and the clientele they serve, there were surprising similarities in their relationships with congressional committees. Clashing with congressional committees was unavoidable, but these disputes, even those that were very intense and salient, did not disrupt decision-making processes. Furthermore, the types of disputes that arose were those of the policy model. Legislators sustained considerable interest in the agencies' administrative actions. They aggressively advanced their demands by complaining about agency management practices, intervening in decisions on specific issues, and attacking the underpinnings of the agencies' programs. The agencies often found themselves on the defensive, trying to fend off or stall these attacks. But they still tried to present their views of good public policy, refusing to acquiesce to all congressional guidelines.

The findings of this research imply that conflict between bureaucrats and legislators is desirable because it results from each institution providing valuable and valid contributions to policy making. Conflict is not disruptive; it does not create sharp and polarized divisions that spill over a variety of issues. Nor does conflict mean that the legislature has little or no control over the bureaucracy. To the contrary, the legislature has the upper hand in these struggles. In fact, granting the legislature greater power could crush the bureaucracy, preventing it from supplementing and balancing the positions of the legislature.

Notes

1. Woodrow Wilson, "The Study of Administration"; Paul Appleby, *Morality and Administration in Democratic Government*; Frederick C. Mosher, *Democracy and the Public Service*; and Emmette S. Redford, *Democracy in the Administrative State*.

2. James Madison, *Federalist Papers*, No. 51.

3. Jerome Frank, *Courts on Trial*, pp. 80–102.

4. Randall B. Ripley and Grace A. Franklin, *Congress, the Bureaucracy, and Public Policy*, p. 241.

5. Morris P. Fiorina, *Congress: The Keystone of the Washington Establishment*, pp. 39–40. A mainstay of the literature arguing that the primary goal of the bureaucracy is to maximize its budget is William Niskanen, *Bureaucracy and Representative Government*.

6. Nicholas Masters, "Committee Assignments in the House of Representatives"; and Steven Smith and Christopher Deering, *Committees in Congress*, pp. 240–243.

7. Steven Smith and Christopher Deering, *Committees in Congress*, pp. 105–106.

8. Anthony Downs outlines the pressures on bureaucrats to become advocates in *Inside Bureaucracy*, pp. 103–107. The tendency of administrators to "marry the natives" is described by Hugh Heclo in *A Government of Strangers*.

9. Compare David Mayhew, *Congress: The Electoral Connection* with Fiorina, *Congress: The Keystone of the Washington Establishment*.

10. Mayhew, *Congress: The Electoral Connection*, pp. 49–73.

11. Theodore J. Lowi, *The End of Liberalism: The Second Republic of the United States*.

12. Lawrence C. Dodd and Richard L. Schott, *Congress and the Administrative State*, pp. 165–184.

13. Daniel McCool, "Subgovernments and the Impact of Policy Fragmentation and Accommodation," p. 264.

14. Arthur Maass, *Muddy Waters: The Army Engineers and the Nation's Rivers*; Douglass Cater, *Power in Washington*; John E. Chubb, *Interest Groups and the Bureaucracy: The Politics of Energy*; J. Leiper Freeman, *The Political Process*; and Ripley and Franklin, *Congress, the Bureaucracy, and Public Policy*.

15. Ripley and Franklin, *Congress, the Bureaucracy, and Public Policy*, pp. 8–10.

16. Theodore J. Lowi, "American Business and Public Policy, Case Studies and Political Theory," pp. 677–695.

17. Ripley and Franklin, *Congress, the Bureaucracy, and Public Policy*, pp. 100–101.

18. Ibid., p. 21; Roger H. Davidson and Walter J. Oleszek, *Congress and Its Members*, pp. 412–414; and Kenneth J. Meier, *Politics and the Bureaucracy*, p. 97.

19. Mancur Olson, *The Logic of Collective Action*.

20. Dorothy Buckton James, *The Contemporary Presidency;* and Charles O. Jones, *The United States Congress*, pp. 358–365.

21. Ripley and Franklin, *Congress, the Bureaucracy, and Public Policy*, pp. 24–25.

22. Ibid., p. 145.

23. Thomas L. Gais, Mark A. Peterson, and Jack Walker, "Interest Groups, Iron Triangles and Representative Institutions in American National Government," pp. 161–185.

24. Ripley and Franklin, *Congress, the Bureaucracy, and Public Policy*, pp. 121–123.

25. Ibid., pp. 103–134.

26. Hugh Heclo, "Issue Networks and the Executive Establishment," pp. 87–124.

27. Gais, Peterson, and Walker, "Interest Groups, Iron Triangles and Representative Institutions in American National Government."

28. Ibid., p. 166.

29. McCool, "Subgovernments and the Impact of Policy Fragmentation and Accommodation," pp. 264–287.

30. In addition to Heclo, "Issue Networks and the Executive Establishment," and Gais, Peterson, and Walker, "Interest Groups, Iron Triangles and Representative Institutions in American National Government," see Roger H. Davidson, "Subcommittee Government: New Channels for Policy Making," p. 131; Arthur Maass, *Congress and the Common Good*, pp. 43–44; Paul A. Sabatier, "Knowledge, Policy-Oriented Learning, and Policy Change: An Advocacy Coalition Framework," pp. 649–692; and Meier, *Politics and the Bureaucracy*, p. 50.

31. McCool, "Subgovernments and the Impact of Policy Fragmentation and Accommodation."

32. Kenneth Shepsle and Barry Weingast, "Legislative Politics and Budget Outcomes," p. 351.

33. Jack Walker, "Setting the Agenda in the U.S. Senate: A Theory of Problem Selection," pp. 423–445.

34. Charles O. Jones, *Clean Air: The Policies and Politics of Pollution Control*.

35. *Congressional Quarterly Weekly Report*, January 24, 1987, pp. 143–144.

36. John Kingdon, *Agendas, Alternatives, and Public Policies*, p. 65.

37. Walker, "Setting the Agenda in the U.S. Senate," pp. 436–437.

38. Charles S. Bullock III, "U.S. Senate Committee Assignments, Preferences, Motivations, and Success," p. 791.

39. David C. Morrison, "A Savvy 500-Pound Gorilla Moves In," *National Journal*, November 15, 1986, p. 2778.

40. James Sundquist, *The Decline and Resurgence of Congress*, pp. 199–272.

41. Louis Fisher, "Judicial Misjudgments about the Lawmaking Process: The Legislative Veto Case," pp. 705–711, and "One Year After *INS* v. *Chadha*: Congressional and Judicial Developments."

42. Barry R. Weingast and Mark J. Moran, "Bureaucratic Discretion or Congressional Control? Regulatory Policymaking by the Federal Trade Commission," pp. 765–800.

43. Downs, *Inside Bureaucracy*, pp. 5–6, 237–246; Rufus Miles, Jr., "The Origin and Meaning of Miles' Law," pp. 399–403.

44. Marver Bernstein, *Regulating Business by Independent Commission*. I do not test this hypothesis here. It merely provides a starting point for an agency's policy goals. Also, a common assumption is that many programs have vague legislative mandates and unclear guidelines. The question of how an agency deals with such a problem when it first starts to administer a program is an interesting question that is not addressed here.

45. R. Shep Melnick, *Regulation and the Courts*, pp. 71–112.

46. Philip Selznick, *TVA and the Grassroots*.

47. Meier, *Politics and the Bureaucracy*, pp. 157–158.

48. Suzanne Weaver, "Antitrust Division of the Department of Justice," in James Q. Wilson, *The Politics of Regulation*, pp. 134–135.

49. Personal interviews with administrators. These executives loved to point out that because I grew up in northern Minnesota, I could not possibly understand this need for water.

50. Marc Allen Eisner and Kenneth J. Meier, "Presidential Control versus

Bureaucratic Power: Explaining the Reagan Revolution in Antitrust," pp. 269–287.

51. Richard Cyert and James March, *A Behavioral Theory of the Firm*; Serge Taylor, *Making Bureaucracies Think*; and Paul A. Sabatier, "Knowledge, Policy-Oriented Learning, and Policy Change," pp. 649–692.

52. Paul A. Sabatier, "An Advocacy Coalition Framework of Policy Change and the Role of Policy-Oriented Learning Therein," pp. 151–157.

53. Matthew Holden, "Imperialism in Bureaucracy," pp. 943–951.

54. William Bruce Wheeler and Michael McDonald, *TVA and the Tellico Dam*, pp. 4–16.

55. I do not wish to imply here that bureaucratic missions never change. If bureaucrats hold policy goals, changing an agency's mission would be a difficult, but not impossible, task. What happens in an agency that has to alter its mission for whatever reason—because it has accomplished its original task or because of political opposition—is an intriguing question.

56. James Q. Wilson, *The Investigators: Managing FBI and Narcotics Agents*, p. 170.

57. Martha Derthick, *Uncontrollable Spending for Social Services Grants*, p. 18.

58. Susan Rasky, "Senate Factions Search for Way to Widen Military Role on Drugs," *The New York Times*, Friday, May 13, 1988, p. 1.

59. Harold Seidman, *Politics, Position, and Power*; and Daniel Patrick Moynihan, *Maximum Feasible Misunderstanding*.

60. Downs, *Inside Bureaucracy*, pp. 158–166.

61. Bruce Heady, "A Typology of Ministers: Implications for Minister–Civil Servant Relationships in Britain," p. 83.

62. *Congressional Quarterly Almanac, 1978*, p. 144.

63. Meier, *Politics and the Bureaucracy*, p. 117.

64. Joel Aberbach, Robert Putnam, and Bert Rockman, *Bureaucrats and Politicians in Western Democracies*, pp. 9–16.

65. This concept of "coupling" comes from the "garbage can" model. See Michael Cohen, James March, and Johan Olsen, "A Garbage Can Model of Organizational Choice," pp. 1–25.

66. This statement may seem absurd, but it is the logical implication of the assumption that the primary goal of bureaucrats is to maximize their budget. It may be worthwhile to contemplate the value of this assumption.

67. Downs, *Inside Bureaucracy*, p. 103.

68. Lawrence Mohr, "The Concept of Organizational Goal," pp. 470–481.

69. Cyert and March, *A Behavioral Theory of the Firm*, pp. 27–29.

70. Herbert Kaufman, *The Forest Ranger*; and Donald Warwick, *A Theory of Public Bureaucracy*, p. 105.

71. Richard F. Fenno, Jr., *Congressmen in Committees*, pp. 1–14.

72. The term oversight is used rather loosely here, emphasizing the criticism of agency management practices that can occur in a variety of forums rather than relying only on a formal oversight investigation. This approach is justified because this study considers legislative review from the perspective of the agencies as well as the committees.

73. Murray Edelman, *The Symbolic Uses of Politics*.

74. Paul J. Quirk, "Food and Drug Administration," in Wilson, *The Politics of Regulation*, pp. 191–235.

2

The Bureau of Reclamation

Those people, when they went in and started to farm there,
had the benefit of long statistics of the U.S. Weather Bureau
showing there is a maximum of only sixty percent of the
water that is needed to properly farm that area. And, at the
present time there is only forty percent. These people, no
doubt, if they are given the benefit of this bill, will be looking
toward Pike's Peak in their spare time to see if they cannot
grow some bananas there, if they can get some Federal money
to help finance the project.[1]
                                    —Representative Craig Hosmer (R–CA)

A black-and-white photo on the wall of an administrator's office portrayed a barren, gray, dusty farm during the Depression era. A sign in front of one of the farm buildings said, "Have faith in God and the U.S. Reclamation." Created in 1902, the Bureau of Reclamation's original mission was to reclaim the arid and semi-arid lands in seventeen western states through irrigation.[2] As the West was settled, the bureau's role was expanded to provide for more diverse water needs. The bureau provides water for farms, industries, and cities, and its multipurpose projects involve generation of hydroelectric power, control of flooding, maintenance of water quality, and the protection of wildlife and fish habitats.

The initial years of the bureau were caught up in the settlement of the West, and the agency focused primarily on irrigation for agricultural purposes. Related to homesteading, the authorizing law specified that an owner could receive irrigated water for only 160 acres of land. The sanctity of the family farm and the role of the bureau in "making the desert bloom" helped create the respected position that the bureau held for many years.

In 1906 Congress amended the reclamation law to allow the bureau to produce hydroelectric power. The Hoover Dam, constructed in 1928, was the first major power-producing dam in the West. This dam also marked the beginning of the construction of large, multipurpose projects by the federal government. In 1939 the bureau was granted formal authority to include in any project plans for municipal and industrial water, irrigation, flood control, navigation, and hydroelectric power production.

Although the 1906 and 1939 laws granted the bureau the authority to produce power and construct multipurpose projects, the bureau's involvement in such projects did not escape controversy. Government production of power was opposed by many who believed that the private sector could produce power more efficiently and who preferred a smaller, less involved, more decentralized federal government. The debate over the appropriate role of the federal government that began with the public production of power at the Hoover Dam continued in the 1950s and 1960s.

The construction of multipurpose projects also brought tension among the various beneficiaries of bureau projects. This tension was exacerbated by the privileged position of irrigation in comparison with municipal and industrial users. The Bureau of Reclamation (BOR) charges irrigation users for the water they receive from bureau projects, but the users pay only what they can afford, and they do not pay interest charges. The other primary users of water and power, municipalities and industries, are charged with interest. Deciding who will pay and how much they will pay are important and often conflictual issues in the planning and administration of bureau projects.

The programs of the Bureau of Reclamation are clearly distributive policy. Interest groups favoring reclamation, such as the local chapters of the Chamber of Commerce and the local water districts, have always lobbied in support of the water projects. Supporters defend the program against attacks that it is quintessential pork barrel by arguing that their activities are not subsidized because costs to the treasury are repaid by the beneficiaries. But the bureau provides water at prices below the market rate, and the true cost of these projects to the nation's taxpayers is often hidden. Potential opponents are dispersed across the nation and were not often represented until the environmental movement began in the 1970s.

Because the Bureau of Reclamation administers distributive policy, we would expect its relationship with the House and Senate Interior committees to fit closely with the self-interest model and the subgovernment variant. Little or no conflict would develop. The committees and the bureau would agree to support the expansion of the agency's programs. Conflict, in the rare event that it occurred, would be raised by outsiders trying to force the consideration of an issue that the subgovernment persistently ignored. This conflict would be disruptive, challenging the foundation of the subgovernment, and forcing it to adapt or disintegrate.

The relationship between the Bureau of Reclamation and the House and Senate Interior committees does not fit the description provided by the self-interest model very well. The policy model provides a clearer understanding of their interactions. Intense conflict developed because the committees were reluctant to support bureau projects, even proposals that were consistent with previous reclamation policies. These conflicts were not raised only by outsiders; committee members responded to and reflected the same issues that caught the eye of reclamation opponents. Finally, conflict was not disruptive. The system could move easily from conflict to consensus and back again because disputes were confined to the issue at hand.

Conflicts over Limits on Reclamation

The Bureau of Reclamation encountered intense conflicts with the House and Senate Interior committees in the 1960s. The committees did not behave like those of the self-interest model; these conflicts are more consistent with the policy model. The disputes arose because the committees were reluctant to endorse the bureau's projects. They wanted the bureau proposals to be consistent with their own policy positions. Unfortunately for the agency, there was little it could do to minimize the opposition in the House and Senate Interior committees.

Reclamation as "Big Government"

In the early 1960s congressional opposition to three bureau projects erupted. One ideological issue—the appropriate role of the federal government—plagued all three proposals. Although this question had been settled before, it reappeared along with the resurgence of the Republican party and was placed on the public agenda by the Eisenhower Administration. It remained on the agenda after the Democrats regained control of the government because members of the House Interior Committee refused to support the projects.

The Bureau of Reclamation presented three projects that were not traditional reclamation proposals. As multipurpose projects, the projects did much more than provide water for agriculture. Burns Creek would have constructed a reservoir and powerplant on the Snake River in Idaho, and Knowles Dam would have provided for the marketing of power in Montana. The Waurika project in Montana was not to create and sell power, but it annoyed many because its primary purpose was to provide water for municipal and industrial users, with only a slight focus on irrigation and flood control.

The House Interior Committee blocked all three projects, even after they were removed from its jurisdiction in an effort to get them passed. Initially, the House Interior Committee did not report any of the bills and specifically voted not to report the Burns Creek legislation. In an attempt to bypass this opposition, the three projects were shifted to the Army Corps of Engineers and added to the rivers and harbors bill by the Public Works Committee in 1962. Although the Senate passed this bill, the projects were dropped again at the insistence of the House. The opposition came from members of the House Interior Committee. These legislators started to act like outsiders—they continued to fight against the projects even though they were no longer in their committee's domain. Representative John Saylor (R–PA), ranking minority member of the House Interior Committee who seemed to see his role as keeping everyone honest, blocked a move to send the bill to conference. When the bill was reconsidered in 1963, the Senate again included the proposals. But the bill never went to conference because at least twenty representatives objected to a unanimous consent bill in the House. Finally, a new bill that authorized the Waurika project but not the Burns Creek or the Knowles Dam projects was submitted and eventually passed.

These three reclamation projects were controversial because they were framed in ideological terms. The central issue was what should be the appropriate role of the federal government. There was a stable consensus on the original purpose of the bureau, irrigating desert land in order to settle the West with family farms. But the multipurpose projects raised questions because they emphasized new functions, the public marketing of power and the provision of municipal and industrial water. Debates, both in committee and on the floor, centered on deviating from traditional reclamation law. In the opponents' eyes, unwarranted subsidies to other water users indicated interference by the federal government in the private sector and only enlarged the national debt. The issue was the role of the federal government, and reclamation was seen as a prime example of big government interfering with free enterprise.[3]

These issues had arisen earlier and had supposedly been settled. Constructing hydroelectric dams along with bureau irrigation projects was not new. The Hoover Dam, the bureau's pride and joy, had been authorized as the first multipurpose project in 1928.[4] In 1939 the Reclamation Act recognized and encouraged multipurpose projects in general.[5] By proposing the three projects, the BOR was continuing policies that had earlier been endorsed by Congress.

Reservations about these policies rose with the resurgence in the 1950s of the more general debate over the provision of power by the public rather than the private sector. This discussion was sparked by the Eisenhower Administration's policy of pressing for the private development of water projects and encompassed the programs of a variety of agencies, including the Army Corps of Engineers, the Federal Power Commission, and the Bonneville Power Administration.[6] The ideological nature of the debate is illustrated by the lines separating supporters and opponents. The cleavage on these issues was partisan, an unusual occurrence for reclamation, where divisions tended to be along geographical lines. Relevant roll-call votes in the House in 1961 and 1962 demonstrate this partisanship, with an average of seventy-seven percent of the Democrats supporting the changes and eighty-nine percent of the Republicans opposing them. Even westerners opposed the altered program.

This ideological dispute did not force the subgovernment to adapt or face disintegration because it did not carry over to other projects. The system was not tightly coupled as in the self-interest model. More traditional reclamation projects were accepted easily by the House and Senate committees in the early 1960s. These projects were adopted with little fanfare. Interest groups, the House and Senate Interior committees, and the Bureau of Reclamation agreed on the program's purposes and praised each project as it came up for authorization. Negotiations among committee members and bureau representatives smoothed out details before the bills reached the floor of each chamber, and the chamber deferred to the expertise of the subgovernment and adopted the bills.

The dispute had the *potential* to carry over to other projects. No new reclamation projects were authorized in 1961.[7] Conflict over the Burns Creek project was intense enough to postpone action on two other projects given high priority by Secretary of the Interior Stewart Udall as well as the chairmen of the House and Senate Interior committees.[8] There was also more criticism of reclamation than there had been in the "Golden Era" of reclamation, the 1940s and 1950s. Committee members from competing agricultural areas fretted over the cheap water the western states received. In committee hearings, for example, Representative Odin Langen (R–MN) often asked witnesses about growing potatoes on the land that would be newly irrigated.[9] Republican committee members continued to rail about the national debt and the low interest rates. In a bit of hyperbole, Representative Craig Hosmer (R–CA) said the low interest rates were a "salami technique toward national bankruptcy" which would hand the United States over to Khrushchev.[10]

The committees were able to handle these complaints through the simple techniques of majority rule and compromise, and the issues remained loosely coupled. The concerns of the competitive agricultural areas were handled easily by committee amendments prohibiting the use of water for ten years on new productive land that would grow surplus crops. The allegations of the Republicans were ignored because they were not the majority party. They did not control the committees or the Congress, and they could not get enough votes from western Republicans to halt traditional reclamation projects.

The Lower Colorado River Basin Project

By 1965 the quarrel over public power had faded away, and another project became embroiled in controversy. This project, the Lower Colorado River Basin Project (CAP), was the center of several fights.[11] On its face, CAP seemed straightforward. The project would transport water from the Colorado River east to the growing metropolitan areas of Phoenix and Tucson, Arizona. But the Colorado River, originating in northern Colorado and flowing southwest through the Grand Canyon, is a major source of surface water for many states in this area as well as Mexico, and CAP could not be considered without also debating the use of water in the entire river basin.

The first dispute, over the decision to authorize CAP, developed because the subgovernment had to grapple with the problem of scarce resources. The bureau's proposal was blocked in Congress not because legislators were annoyed with the BOR but because they could not resolve their own differences. This conflict illustrates the difficulty of maintaining a supportive coalition even in a prototypical subgovernment. The struggle highlights the diversity of interests and the divisions among the western states, the need to have enough resources to satisfy all the demands, and the constraints on agency strategies to build legislative support. This controversy almost shattered the reclamation subgovernment because it involved a split among congressional supporters that threatened to carry over to other water projects. The alliance was weakened, but like the fight over public power, the dispute was confined to the issue at hand.

When the Lower Colorado River Basin Project was finally authorized in 1968, it ended, at least temporarily, more than forty years of squabbling among the seventeen western states. There was congressional support for CAP, but there was also a great deal of opposition, most of which came from western states. The deadlock that delayed the project was not caused by an eastern–western division, but by a division within the subgovernment, a division between California and Arizona, between the upper Colorado Basin states and the lower Colorado Basin states, and between the Pacific northwestern states and the southwestern states. Usually, these differences in a subgovernment are reconciled before a bill is introduced or reported from the committee. Such a process did not work well for the Basin Project. The projected shortage of water in the Colorado River Basin heightened competition for water among the reclamation states. With each state pushing for its own interests and a lack of resources to satisfy all, compromise was difficult to achieve.

In 1922 the Colorado River compact evenly divided all the waters of the river between the upper basin (Colorado, Utah, Wyoming, and New Mexico) and the lower basin (California, Nevada, and Arizona). Attempts to enact CAP began in 1947, and the Senate passed authorization bills in 1949 and 1951. Legislative efforts halted, however, in 1952 after the House Interior Committee decided that further consideration of CAP should be delayed until the dispute between the lower basin states could be resolved. Arizona and California could not agree on how the lower basin states' share of the water should be divided. Arizona filed suit against California in 1952, the case was decided in

1963, and legislative initiatives were resumed in 1964.

The major obstacle to the enactment of CAP stemmed from the disagreements among the reclamation states about what should be included in the project. The lower basin states wanted to adopt a national approach to the basin. Under such an approach, the United States' obligation to deliver water to Mexico as specified in the 1944 Mexican Water Treaty would be a national obligation. All states would be responsible for making sure that Mexico received the water it was entitled to. Ways to augment the Colorado River's water supply would also be studied. However, the upper basin states, along with California, thought the Mexican Treaty should be a regional obligation, one that did not require their contributions. The Pacific northwestern states feared the importation of water from the Columbia and Snake rivers to the Colorado River and opposed any provisions to authorize the Bureau of Reclamation to study this possibility.

Particular states also specified their own requirements. California refused to support the project unless Arizona agreed to provisions guaranteeing California its share of water, 4.4 million acre feet per year, even in times of shortage.[12] Wayne Aspinall (D–CO), chairman of the House Interior Committee, did not support the project because he feared that Colorado and the other upper basin states would not receive their fair share of the river's water. A question Aspinall repeatedly asked during 1965 hearings was what would happen if there were a water shortage, not an unlikely event. Morris Udall (D–AZ), a primary supporter of CAP, could not get committee approval of the bill without Aspinall's support. In order to obtain Aspinall's endorsement, five projects in Colorado were added to the authorization, three of which the Bureau of the Budget opposed.

The Bureau of Reclamation was drawn into the dispute even though the complaints were not aimed directly at the agency. During the hearings, members grumbled some about the changing positions of the bureau and the Department of Interior, but they criticized neither the bureau's programs nor its procedures. However, the bureau found CAP, a project it wanted to construct, stymied in Congress for five years because the committees could not find a consensus position. Unfortunately for the agency, there was nothing it could do to build this consensus. Any action it took, even inaction, would have upset an important segment of the House and Senate Interior committees. If it endorsed a national approach to the Mexican Water Treaty, it would annoy the upper basin states. It could support a regional approach only by disturbing the lower basin states. The agency wanted to study increasing the water supply, but if it pressed this solution, it would arouse the Pacific northwestern states, who believed that the southern states had their eyes on the water of the Columbia and Snake rivers. Because the various demands conflicted with each other, the bureau had no conflict-minimizing strategy it could productively adopt. Resolution of the issue had to stem from the legislators themselves.

The debate over the project continued until 1968. In 1965 a solution seemed imminent when California and Arizona reconciled their differences by agreeing that existing projects in California, Nevada, and Arizona would have a higher priority than CAP during periods of water shortage. This unified front, however, was tenuous, and feathers were easily ruffled. Although members of Congress applauded the alliance, it collapsed in 1966 when California withdrew its support of the proposal while the bill was in the House Rules Committee. California members were displeased with the Interior Committee's decision to downgrade the study of water diversion from a feasibility to a reconnaissance study because they felt the downgrade indicated that water diversion was not viewed as a serious policy option.[13] Representative Edwin Reinecke (R–CA) claimed that the California delegation had been "hoodwinked."[14] There were also concerns that the committee could not maintain control over the bill on the floor. Representatives were afraid that the bill would not be adopted without amendments and that the substitute bill introduced by Saylor (R–PA), a member of the Interior Committee, would be passed.

In 1968, a compromise was finally attained, essentially by ignoring the problem that had caused the controversy in the first place, the lack of water to meet everyone's demands. Henry Jackson (D–WA) secured the support of the Pacific northwestern states by pushing for a ten-year moratorium on studies of the importation of water. The northwestern states were assured that their rivers were safe from the conniving minds of other states.[15] Aspinall received authorization for the projects in Colorado, and California was guaranteed its allotted share of water even in years of shortage. The compromise among the states that allowed the project to be adopted ignored the fact that there was a scarcity of resources, that there would not be enough water to satisfy all of the participants' demands once all of the projects were completed.

The other central controversy that swirled around CAP portended controversies that would emerge in the 1970s. Until this time Congress had made few attempts to require BOR to weigh environmental impacts when designing projects. Consistent with past policy, the BOR proposed projects with little consideration of their environmental consequences. In this case, however, the committees buckled to the demands that natural resources should be preserved.

To ensure the financial feasibility of CAP, two hydroelectric dams, the Bridge, or Hualapai, and Marble Canyon dams, were included in the Interior Department's initial proposal. The power from these dams would be marketed, and the revenues deposited in a basin account to pay for other provisions of the project. Because the two dams would have affected forty miles of the Grand Canyon National Monument and thirteen miles of the National Park,[16] the Sierra Club targeted the two dams for defeat. Its full-page advertisements in the *New York Times* and other newspapers claimed the dams would turn the Grand Canyon into a cash register. Borrowing a term used by the Bureau of Reclamation to promote the dams, the advertisements warned of the commercialization of the Grand Canyon, and they generated numerous complaints. As a result of the controversy, the Bureau of the Budget withdrew its recommendation of the Bridge Canyon Dam in 1965 and asked that a decision be deferred pending a study. The administration dropped the Bridge Canyon Dam in 1966 and the Marble Canyon Dam in 1967.[17] A thermal electric generating plant in Page, Arizona, was substituted to fund CAP.

Initially, the committees and the bureau both agreed on the proposal for the two dams. The bureau supported the dams, and the bill reported out of the House Interior Committee in 1966 included plans for them. However, this consensus faltered as the committees, responding to external pressures and internal dissent, dropped the two dams from the proposal. The bureau continued to support the dams even after the administration withdrew its endorsement. The bureau had to go along with that position officially, but it was public knowledge that it wanted the dams authorized.

Both the House and Senate committees quickly followed the lead of the administration. The Marble Dam, the dam that would have directly affected the Grand Canyon, was dropped quietly by both the House and the Senate committees shortly after the administration withdrew its support. A position on the second dam, Bridge Canyon, was not reached so quickly. But both the Senate and the House Interior committees reported out bills in 1967 and 1968, respectively, that did not include provisions for this dam. The Senate committee acted more decisively than the House committee when it rejected a substitute bill that included the dam by a four-to-twelve vote in 1967. In the House committee a persistent minority led by John Saylor (R–PA) unsuccessfully tried to delete the dam in 1966.[18] They finally succeeded in 1968.

In this dispute the importance of actors outside the subgovernment cannot be denied. But these "outsiders" did not have a difficult time raising their concerns. The environmentalists found a symbol to use against the projects that appealed to the mass public. The administration's about-face was followed by the committees without a fight. Facing the opposition of the president and the environmentalists, the committees knew they could not pass a proposal including the two dams.

These "outsiders" succeeded rather easily because they were not exactly outsiders. The pattern of events suggests that, at least in the House committee, the majority of members were not opposed to the dams per se. But a significant minority of the committee members were concerned about the environmental issues, and they managed to block the projects. Although it is difficult to uncover views of individual committee members, votes on the Hooker Dam—another part of the Lower Colorado River Basin Project—indicate concern about environmental protection. Seventeen members of the House committee filed additional views to the committee report expressing their opposition to the Hooker Dam because of its environmental consequences.[19] The majority knew that without a united front on the floor, the committee could not overcome the opposition and win on the floor. The committees capitulated to their internal dissension and altered the bills so that they were acceptable to the other legislators.

Reflecting on these disputes of the 1960s, it becomes apparent that they do not fit with the hypotheses of the self-interest model but are consistent with the policy model. First, the opposition of the committees to the projects follows from the hypotheses of the policy model. The self-interest model predicts that the authorizing committees would endorse, not oppose, the bureau's program. The goal of reelection is supposed to drive legislators to endorse pork-barrel projects and to adopt decision rules that enable all members to acquire the projects they think they need.[20] Agencies that advocated additional projects would seldom, if ever, encounter opposition from congressional committees. In these instances, however, the Bureau of Reclamation proposed projects that were consistent with past policies, yet the Interior committees rejected some of them and were very reluctant to endorse the others.

Second, the self-interest model predicts that conflictual issues would be raised by actors outside of the subgovernment. Because these actors, such as interest groups and the president, cannot persuade the committees to address their concerns, they must resort to external strategies, such as raising the issue on the floor of Congress. However, the disputes involving the Bureau of Reclamation suggest that subgovernments are permeable, which fits with the hypotheses of the policy model. Because the views of committee members were diverse, new issues were raised rather easily in the committees. The distributive policy of water projects was transformed to an ideological question—the public marketing of power—when that issue was raised by a Republican president. The problem of environmental protection was taken seriously by a significant portion of the committees. The subgovernment had a difficult time resolving the problem of resource scarcity, resulting in an intense and protracted battle over CAP.

Third, the self-interest model predicts that conflict disrupts the standard practice of decision making. Because the relationships are somewhat brittle, a challenge can snap the consensus and permanently alter the pattern of the interactions among the actors. The policy model allows for a more fluid and dynamic shift from conflict to consensus, and the history of the reclamation subgovernment suggests that this more resilient and isolated response to conflict is possible. The debate over CAP was confined to that issue, although several members admonished that they would withhold their support for other projects until CAP was passed.[21] The ideological and party conflict over the construction of hydroelectric dams in the early 1960s did not spread to other types of bureau projects. Even though these were conflicts that centered on fundamental issues in water policy, the subgovernment was not forced to adapt or disintegrate. To the contrary, the committees were able to settle the disputes without allowing them to spill over to other issues.

Conflicts over Program Retrenchment

In the late 1970s and early 1980s, the consensus between the bureau and the committees was threatened by concerns that seemed more difficult to confine to particular issues. Doubts about cost required a justification of the entire reclamation program rather than just a few of the projects. The question of environmental protection versus resource development encompassed almost all dams and irrigation projects. These issues were not really new; the subgovernment had grappled with them before. But they were different because they were joined together in a general attack on reclamation.

Following the outlines of the self-interest model, Randall B. Ripley and Grace A. Franklin assert that the water subgovernment adapted to pressures from external actors.[22] Although their account captures some of what has happened in reclamation policy, the perspective is incomplete. Consistent with the policy model, a considerable amount of opposition to the reclamation program came from within the subgovernment. Responding to policy concerns, legislators on both the House and Senate committees used their positions to advance their views about the reclamation program. The subgovernment was not forced by outsiders to adapt; insiders readily acknowledged these policy concerns.

In light of these attacks, the Bureau of Reclamation tried to maintain its construction program and prevent the transformation of its program from construction to merely operation and maintenance of existing projects. However, the agency did not fight to protect its program as strongly as one might expect. The bureau adjusted its policy views, albeit more slowly than the committees, by responding to demands for greater environmental protection. In addition, because of scarce resources, the bureau had few strategies it could use to maintain a supportive coalition in Congress.

Environmental Protection, Cost Sharing, and Reclamation

From 1976 to 1985, only one new water project, the Buffalo Bill Dam, was authorized.[23] Proposals for projects were introduced, but they were not reported out of committee. Large-scale projects were simply out of the question. One committee staff member called this a "major departure from historical practice" and said that "most projects with a $1 billion price tag have no chance at all. If a bill costs $200 million, there won't even be a mark-up because the project sponsors are afraid they're going to lose. The evolution of reclamation is moving it away from development into management."[24] Some members pushed for projects that they felt their areas justly deserved because of past sacrifices, but little action was taken. For example, Senator James Abdnor (R–SD) lobbied for irrigation projects in South Dakota to compensate for the flooding of prime farmland by dams built on the Missouri River to control flooding downstream. This notion of "getting my fair share" was a common justification for supporting water projects and was honored in the past. However, bureaucrats and committee staff members felt that these projects would not be adopted even though supporters claimed there was a legal obligation, if not a moral one, to construct them.

Committee members were reluctant to advance project proposals as they became more concerned about environmental protection and the federal deficit. "People have started to ask, why should we spend money on a big water project," commented one staff member.[25] Another expressed the same idea with more emotion:

> In the heydays, four or five congressmen would get together and decide who gets what. And now, the first thing they look at is if it's absolutely, positively necessary, if it's do or die, if it's national security. Well, this is a water project. The demagogues say that this is a project to get more water to fill hot tubs in California, swimming pools in Arizona. That doesn't fly well. Water projects now are very expensive. It cost about $200 million for the Hoover Dam. It would probably cost $200 billion to build today. There's even more of this in the last two or three years.[26]

In the 1980s environmentalists discovered they could increase the impact of their argument by joining with fiscal conservatives and using cost as an argument against projects. Said a staff member, "The environmental movement has discovered that financial issues are better than some obscure duck as a way to block a project, at least with this [the Reagan] Administration."[27] A report published by the National Wildlife Federation, an environmental protection group, focused almost entirely on cost and had only short summaries of the environmental problems created by these projects.[28]

Lack of funds and environmental consequences were not the only barriers to committee endorsement. States found they were competing for a small supply of water, and an even smaller supply of high-quality water. Those areas that had an adequate supply of water, such as the Pacific northwestern states and northern California, were reluctant to share it with anyone else:

Each state has its own problems. In Arizona it's how to guarantee that they will get the money for their projects. In California it's the north versus the south. There are rivers in northern California that have been locked up, by scenic rivers and such. [Question: What do you mean by locked up?] The rivers can't be developed, the water can't be taken from them for other purposes. There is a direct statement from the north to the south—don't take this water. So they have to develop the rivers that are available.[29]

Those areas that did not have enough water quibbled over the quality of water delivered. Realizing that the demand for water throughout the West was high, states that still had supplies of undeveloped water hoarded what water they had the legal right to but were not using:

There is some necessary infighting. You know, water has been allocated among those states. Colorado isn't using all of their water, and San Diego came up with a project to send that water to California for their use. San Diego wants the excess water shipped to them. But Colorado said, no you're not going to get our water, even though they're not using it.[30]

Facing these scarce resources, members often found that they were competing against each other rather than building a supportive coalition that could adopt the projects of all members.

When a bill finally made it to the floor of the House or Senate, the bill's sponsors could not count on support from committee members. Support for bureau projects from committee members could be attained, but it could no longer be assumed. Members did not automatically support continued funding for particular projects that were constantly criticized, like the Garrison Diversion Unit in North Dakota or the O'Neill Unit in the Missouri River Basin. Smaller projects that earlier might have been passed easily under a suspension of the rules were not always supported. If compromises were made to satisfy opponents, support from the committee increased.

Table 2.1 presents the average percentage of committee members voting in favor of reclamation on a series of roll-call votes from 1961 to 1984.[31] The low percentages in the Eighty-seventh and Eighty-eighth Congresses reflect the disputes over the public marketing of power. From 1965 to 1975, there was stable and high support for reclamation programs. With the Ninety-fourth Congress, committee

Table 2.1

**Average Percentage of Committee Members Voting in Support of
Reclamation, 1961 to 1984, 87th Congress to 98th Congress**

	House Interior Committee		Senate Interior Committee	
Congress	Percent	Number of Votes	Percent	Number of Votes
87	58	4	81	5
88	73	4	69	4
89	88	6	62	1
90	95	5	25[a]	1
91	—	0	—	0
92	100	1	—	0
93	92	2	81	5
94	80	8	—	0
95	71	8	57	6
96	65	10	68	9
97	54	9	72	6
98	79	8	73	6

Source: These votes were coded from the *Congressional Quarterly Almanac*, volumes dated from 1961 to 1984.

[a]This vote is on a substitute to the Interior Committee's bill authorizing CAP. The substitute would have authorized the Hualapai, or Bridge, Canyon Dam and a study of proposals to import water into the Colorado River Basin.

support in the House began to wane until it hit a very low point of fifty-four percent in the Ninety-seventh Congress. Support rose in 1983–84 although it did not return to the very high levels of the late 1960s and early 1970s. The increased support in the Ninety-eighth Congress stemmed from the fact that concessions were made to make the proposals palatable to opponents before the bills came up for consideration on the floor. Starting with the Ninety-fourth Congress there was also an increase in the number of roll-call votes at the same time there was a decrease in the number of projects considered, indicating that it became more difficult to pass proposals with little debate. In the Senate committee there were not enough votes to establish a clear trend. Although support scores did not decline as much as they did in the House committee, support fluctuated more from vote to vote in the late 1970s and early 1980s.

President Carter's widely publicized failure to halt the funding of several projects is often seen as incontrovertible evidence of the solidity and perseverance of the subgovernment. However, Carter's defeat stemmed from the strategy he adopted to cut funds from the projects; he aroused great concern over the institutional strength of Congress and deflected attention away from the issue of environmental protection. The hostile reaction of the legislature to Carter's "hit list" was primarily due to congressional concern over the interference of the president in the authorization process and not because of support for the projects themselves. The issue was one of institutional power, whether the president could use the appropriations process to supersede programs adopted by Congress:

> That thing was viewed as an outpouring of support for the water program, but it was a straight separation of power. . . . The whole thing was calculated to blow up in his face. It wasn't enthusiasm for water programs, it was a gut reaction from people who didn't even give a damn. It was an institutional response from Congress. People were concerned that if he got away with this one, health programs would be next.[32]

If Carter had attacked one project at a time on the basis of its merits, he probably would have been more successful. Both bureau officials and staff members stated that President Reagan essentially continued Carter's approach to the water projects and was more successful in curtailing their funding.

The leadership of the president and the difficulty of maintaining a supportive coalition were apparent to House leaders in the battle over cost sharing, when a good number of committee members defected from the committee's position to follow President Reagan's lead.[33] In 1982 a bill to authorize appropriations for dam safety repairs, one that normally might be considered minor and difficult to vote against, was amended on the House floor to require state and local beneficiaries to pay some of the costs. This adoption of the infamous Solomon amendment shocked leaders on the House Interior Committee, who did not expect to lose, especially by seventy-two votes.[34] But the committee leaders were not able to retain the support of their traditional coalition when the president endorsed the amendment. Twenty-seven percent of House westerners and thirty-nine percent of the members on the House Interior Committee supported the amendment.

When the Reagan Administration reversed its position on the same amendment in 1984, reclamation supporters were able to rebuff attempts to impose cost sharing but only by a two-vote margin. Without the tug of the administration, the straying westerners returned to the fold, and eighty-eight percent of them opposed cost sharing.

Even though the westerners were cohesive on this issue in 1984, the extremely close vote demonstrated to congressional leaders that concessions had to be made to adopt proposals. Senator Howard Metzenbaum (D–OH), a member of the Senate Energy and Natural Resources Committee, held up the dam safety repair bill until westerners agreed to partial cost sharing.[35] Although the percentage of cost sharing was not as high as Metzenbaum might have preferred, the provision established a precedent for other acts. One staff member assumed that it was a bottom line—that future laws would not have a lower cost-sharing rate.[36] The Colorado salinity bill, as passed by the Senate, also had thirty-percent cost sharing.

Because of the divisions within the committees, leaders knew they could not succeed on the floor without making concessions to the program's opponents. Although substantial new projects were not being considered, bills to reauthorize projects, raise appropriation ceilings, or adjust reclamation law still arose. When they did, they faced many more battles. One staff member likened the situation to the story about the three Billy Goats Gruff with Metzenbaum as the troll under the bridge:

> What it amounts to isn't a positive enactment of a policy. But as different projects go by—it's like when billy goats go over the bridge, they'll [reclamation opponents] take a piece out of each goat. We have to get these past him. Metzenbaum is the wall. The Small Reclamation Project Act had to be introduced last year, and it went nowhere. On Colorado salinity, Metzenbaum wanted twenty-five to thirty percent cost sharing; he was under the bridge taking a piece out of it. There will be an increase in the interest rate or the cost sharing, but everything is done on a piecemeal basis. As the West needs legislation and things have to be reauthorized, the easterners will make them pay a toll.[37]

Maintaining the support of committee members to present a united front on the floor was not the only problem encountered by committee leaders. They also had to deal with a more fragile coalition once they turned to the floor. All respondents acknowledged that the coalition of southerners and westerners that traditionally supported the projects of the Bureau of Reclamation and the Corps of Engineers had weakened, although they did not all agree on the extent of this erosion. As was illustrated by the dispute over CAP, there were always divisions among the reclamation states. The problem of scarce resources that led to the fight over CAP was exacerbated in the late 1970s and early 1980s.

Without the resources to satisfy each member's requests, it was difficult to maintain a solid coalition. Legislators had no reason to support the projects in other districts and states if they believed such support would not be returned when their own projects were considered. The notion of "one for you and one for me" was no longer a reliable governing maxim:

> Somewhere along the line the club broke down. There used to be extreme cohesion. Each one knew he was moving up a predetermined line to the check-out counter, and when he got to the cash register, he would get his project. Somewhere along the line, the South–West coalition broke down. Sometimes it works, and sometimes it doesn't. It worked to a certain extent on the Reclamation Reform Act. The way we were able to defeat certain amendments—certain northeastern amendments— was by having the South with us. They had nothing to gain by it, but they were cajoled and encouraged. We'd tell them it was those fag liberals from the northeast. In Tennessee–Tombigbee it worked. Since I've been here, it's been destroyed.[38]

Although enacting reclamation bills has become much more difficult, the committees and the bureau have been able to work out agreement on some bills. Consensus on specific items can be reached despite the conflict over the direction of the reclamation program. In 1982 the Reclamation Reform Act was adopted. The first major reform of reclamation law since 1926, the act had the potential of splitting apart the various supporters of reclamation by raising the same kinds of issues that frustrated CAP in the 1960s. But through slow and patient deliberations, committee members and the agency were able to negotiate a consensus. In 1984 supporters of reclamation succeeded in passing some important bills because their concessions fended off some of the opposition. A program to study recharging the high plains groundwater was authorized with twenty-percent cost sharing. The contracts for power from the Hoover Dam were renegotiated after the House dropped a section that would authorize funds to increase the generating capacity at seven other bureau plants.[39] Language specifying the use of the market interest rate was included in the salinity and the dam safety bills.

As this account demonstrates, opposition to reclamation programs was not raised solely by outsiders forcing a subgovernment to take up issues it wanted to ignore. Much of the opposition came from committee members themselves, as they reacted to concerns about environmental protection, the federal deficit, and competition among the states. Committee members were not isolated from these issues nor did they really try to ignore them. As the policy model indicates, legislators have a variety of reasons to take up, and even search for, these new issues.

The Interior Committees and Environmental Protection

The way in which the House and Senate Interior committees were introduced to and responded to these issues, particularly environmental protection, deserves some consideration. Neither committee was insulated from concerns about environmental degradation. To the contrary, the committees had to deal with the question of environmental protection, because of their jurisdiction as well as their membership.

Reservations about reclamation policies arose partly because of changes in the membership of the Interior committees. Both the House and Senate committees were traditionally staffed by western legislators.[40] With the energy crisis and the environmental movement in the mid-1970s, the committees began to acquire national importance. The make-up of the committees changed dramatically as more easterners became attracted to the new issues that seemed to be more relevant to their constituents.[41] As one staff member grumbled, even a senator from New Jersey could find something in the committee's jurisdiction to please his constituents; he could write a newsletter home about the wonderful improvements he could make in the national parks. In the Ninety-eighth Congress, fifty-five percent of the Senate committee's members were not from one of the seventeen western states, and forty-four percent of the House committee were not westerners (see Table 2.2). The shift in the House committee was slower and steadier than in the Senate, largely because, as a larger body, it had a fair number of easterners even in 1961. In the Senate one of the most vociferous opponents of the reclamation program, Howard Metzenbaum (D–OH), even sat on the relevant subcommittee in the Ninety-eighth and Ninety-ninth Congresses.

These changes demonstrate that committees respond to influences

Table 2.2

**Percentage of Committee Members Who Were Not from the Seventeen
Reclamation States, 1961 to 1984, 87th Congress to 98th Congress**

Congress	House Interior Committee Percent	Senate Interior Committee Percent
87	32	24
88	36	12
89	39	12
90	39	12
91	39	18
92	37	12
93	41	15
94	38	29
95	46	39
96	40	56
97	44	65
98	44	55

Source: Data were collected from the *Congressional Quarterly Almanac*, volumes dated
from 1961 to 1984.

from the chamber through membership shifts. It has usually been assumed that certain committees attract legislators with particular and
similar goals. But there is little, except perhaps the stability of policy
debates, to prevent committee membership from changing. Easterners
were attracted to the Interior committees because of energy and environmental issues, not because of reclamation. Gradually, however,
they became more interested in and knowledgeable of water resource
issues. The effect of the movement of committee members is that
outsiders became insiders. Even if only one legislator such as Senator
Metzenbaum devoted considerable attention to reclamation, his position on the committee granted legitimacy to his resistance and provided leadership for the opponents. Sometimes he would lose in
committee, but his actions there allowed him to use parliamentary
maneuvers on the floor to demand concessions.[42]

Declining support for reclamation was not due only to the influx of
easterners on the committees. Respondents recognized that committee
members from the West were different than they were fifteen years
ago. Even in the West the new issues became more critical and dis-
placed reclamation:

Before that, reclamation had a life of its own. When there were important people interested in it, it would just go. It became less significant
even for those people. For [Senator Henry] Jackson in the early days,
reclamation was important for constituency relations and re-election.
Then gas lines became much more salient. Reclamation fell in significance even to its own home front.[43]

With other issues catching the attention of members, the number of
experts like Aspinall (D–CO) and Jackson (D–WA), who had earlier
reigned over the program, diminished:

The new Senators don't know anything about the program. If you look
at the ones who came after 1968–69 or maybe even after 1965, they
couldn't even answer a true or false test with reasonable questions
about things like repayment. The ones who had been with the program
and built it—Jackson, Church, Anderson, and Aspinall—are all gone.
None of them are left. They lived with it in the heyday. Now they [the
new Senators] never understood why we were doing it in the first
place.[44]

Western legislators as well as easterners did not ignore the environmental issues. In fact, through the Interior committees they had to
confront them because their jurisdiction encompassed a variety of environmental programs. The Interior committees have jurisdiction over
the national wilderness program, the national park system, and the wild
and scenic rivers system, and they actively promoted these programs.
A series of roll-call votes on environmental issues from 1961 to 1984
(Table 2.3) illustrates the considerable support members provided for
environmental protection. Even when environmental protection
clashed with water development, members did not necessarily support
the water projects. In 1976 seventy-nine percent of the House committee and sixty-nine percent of the Senate committee voted to include the New River as part of the wild and scenic rivers system and
to invalidate a Federal Power Commission license to construct a hydroelectric power project. In 1978 members rebuffed attempts to further weaken the Endangered Species Act and provide exceptions to
certain types of projects. On three votes in the Senate, an average of
eighty-two percent of the Energy and Natural Resources Committee
voted against these amendments.

Despite the desire to support both environmental protection and

Table 2.3

Average Percentage of Committee Members Voting in Support of Environmental Protection, 1961 to 1984, 87th Congress to 98th Congress

	House Interior Committee		Senate Interior Committee	
Congress	Percent	Number of Votes	Percent	Number of Votes
87	80	5	71	5
88	68	2	82	1
89	59	8	75	4
90	63	5	60	1
91	78	2	62	3
92	58	15	47	13
93	55	15	68	19
94	60	25	58	22
95	68	21	73	13
96	67	14	55	23
97	63	11	47	4
98	62	16	—	0

Source: These votes were coded from the *Congressional Quarterly Almanac*, volumes dated from 1961 to 1984.

water resource development, members were confronted with the need to make trade-offs. Initially, reconciling environmental protection with water projects was not too difficult. Projects included plans for recreation areas, fish hatcheries, and fish and wildlife habitats. Supporters of reclamation tried to fend off criticisms by saying that the projects actually enhanced the environment. When environmental protection conflicted with economic development, members supported compromises and expected others to do the same.

This strategy became problematic when environmental groups were not satisfied with recreation and wanted to protect and preserve the wilderness. Water quality became a serious issue, particularly in the Colorado River Basin where salinity levels increased as more and more water was diverted. The most feasible dam sites were already used, and sites that did not present serious environmental problems were not easy to find. Ironically, the acts that the Interior committees passed to protect the environment were increasingly used to stall reclamation projects:

> Anderson's problem was that he was the architect of the Wilderness Act, and it was used to frustrate a project he held dear. He was con-

vinced that the Wilderness Act hadn't done that, that a reservoir could be allowed. But they used it to stop this project. He felt betrayed, he thought he was part of the wilderness movement, and then they used it against him. Jackson was the principal architect of the National Environmental Policy Act, and he found a fair amount of annoyance at the extent it was used to harass him. He was an old lunch-box Democrat who thought that jobs should be developed. When environmental amenities were supposed to come before economic development in each case, he couldn't buy into it. He understood there was environmental damage, but he didn't follow the mentality. To greater or lesser degrees, the old-time westerners felt that way.[45]

The Bureau's Response

Like the committees, the Bureau of Reclamation also had to confront these environmental concerns. The agency accepted but did not endorse the changes in reclamation. Although many administrators still believed strongly in water development, the agency was forced to change its standard operating procedures in order to be more conscious of environmental consequences. The agency did not aggressively promote environmental protection, but it realized that it would have to adjust to meet these new demands.

The Bureau of Reclamation did not have an easy time coming to grips with the environmental movement. Many bureau personnel believed firmly in the mission to develop the West. Without the BOR's dams, the West would not have been won. Water was the key to continued economic development, and it was the privileged few who could afford to oppose reclamation:

> There is a trade-off between the person who lives in San Francisco, has a lot of money, and can float down the Colorado River and the person who lives by the river and gets flooded out. It's between the opponents, the Sierra Club in New York who says that then they won't be able to look at the last redwood, and the local people who say they have to eat.[46]

Some bureau officials viewed the reclamation program as serving the public interest. The environmental groups were the special interests, and they frustrated the will of the majority:

> What bothers me personally is that the Environmental Protection Act and procedures is used as a tool to stop something. If a minority group in some small community doesn't want the project, they can file suit

and stop it. A small group stops the achievement of a public good for the majority.[47]

Despite this view of the environmental movement, the bureau had to alter its decision-making processes to give greater weight to the environmental consequences of projects. Because the National Environmental Policy Act (NEPA) required agencies to prepare environmental impact statements for major federal actions, reclamation projects had to have prepared statements outlining the effect of the undertaking on the environment. The evaluation of these environmental consequences altered the types of projects sent to and debated by Congress. Some projects were not advanced because of the environmental problems they would have caused. The requirements of NEPA led bureau personnel to be more aware of the environmental effects of projects, even though they did not always want to be. Projects that did not have severe environmental problems were favored over those that did:

> Before NEPA, the commissioner of reclamation didn't think in terms of Project X creating this environmental problem and Project Y having no problem, so we'll go with Project Y. [Now] everybody in the process is aware, so they will say, look at this, this is a real doozy. Then they will push the other one first.[48]

Several other respondents stated that the environmental movement changed the procedures used to authorize projects, that environmental protection was built into the way things were done, and that now "real dogs" could not be authorized.

In addition to the recognition that the opposition's arguments had some validity, the agency's resignation to these changes stemmed from the fact that it could do little else. Even if the BOR wanted to oppose these changes more strenuously, it would be unable to do so because it had few tactics to maintain support. According to R. Douglas Arnold, strategies to build coalitions and minimize conflict for an established program will be led by bureaucrats.[49] Because they have little of value to trade, they try to build support by allocating more benefits to more people. The problem, however, is that this consensus-building strategy depends on an expansion of the available benefits. In a period of restricted resources, this approach meant little to the BOR.

The Bureau of Reclamation has always been in an awkward position to implement a consensus-building strategy because it only operates in seventeen states. Extending its geographical base was out of the question because it would quickly run into the province of the Army Corps of Engineers. Traditionally, this dilemma was handled by the alliance between the southern and western states. However, with few resources, it was difficult to maintain such an alliance. Financial as well as environmental costs were more obvious. Members of the alliance were less willing to support all projects in order to get the specific ones they wanted. Authorizing any project was difficult, and coalition leaders could not act quickly or often enough to push projects for those whose support for water resource development was waning.

An alternative approach would be to fall back on what Arnold labels a general-benefit strategy, discussing the merits of and rationale for the program.[50] For reclamation, the problem with this strategy was that the original justification of the program had largely been met. The program was designed to settle the West and develop its economy. In most areas that has already occurred. In the remaining underdeveloped areas, projects rarely had the positive benefit–cost ratio needed to justify their construction.

Aaron Wildavsky's and Richard F. Fenno's work on budgeting stresses another possible strategy, the importance of interpersonal relationships.[51] According to Wildavsky, trust, honesty, and confidence are critical attributes that bureaucrats should portray to have their requests received favorably by congressional committees. In this study respondents were asked how they would characterize the relationship between the bureau and a particular committee. Almost all stated that it was very good, that they trusted each other and worked well together.[52] However, there seemed to be little connection between the interpersonal relationships and questions of policy. All respondents discussed the tensions and different opinions on policy issues. Good interpersonal relationships may help people finish their tasks, but they will not necessarily resolve important policy differences.

Considering its options, the resignation of the BOR is not surprising. Its main hope was that individual legislators would be able to exert enough influence to prevent some changes from being adopted. For example, Senator Paul Laxalt was credited with persuading the Reagan Administration to reverse its position on cost sharing in 1984. Compared with the other agencies in this study, the BOR would seem to have the best chance of maintaining congressional support because it provides discrete benefits. Its inability to maintain a supportive coalition does not bode well for the other agencies.

Questions of Management

The Bureau of Reclamation was the only one of the four agencies studied that escaped frequent complaints about the agency's management, even during the times when the committees opposed the agency's projects.[53] There were, of course, isolated questions and complaints by individual legislators. But the agency escaped the waves of investigations endured by the Food and Drug Administration, the accusations leveled at the Bureau of Indian Affairs, and the persistent oversight of the Social and Rehabilitation Service.

The absence of complaints about agency management does not mean that the legislators granted discretion to the bureau and then ignored its administrative decisions. In the 1960s, at the beginning of each legislative session, bureau officials met with the committees for a briefing. The 1982 Reclamation Reform Act was preceded by numerous hearings about the enforcement of and problems with existing law. More important, the process used to authorize reclamation projects allowed the most serious problems to be uncovered early. Undesirable projects could be weeded out by the initial reconnaissance studies. Feasibility studies had to be authorized by Congress and reviewed before final approval for construction could be given by Congress. Because of this process, legislators could easily follow the administrative decisions of the BOR.

In the late 1970s and early 1980s, when authorizing projects were generally blocked, one could easily imagine frequent oversight and complaints by the committees. Emphasis on oversight did not develop, however, probably because investigation of the bureau would have yielded outcomes unfavorable to the program's supporters.[54] Although there were certainly opponents of the current reclamation program on the committees, and they developed some strength to block legislation and force compromise, they had not assumed enough control to set the committees' agendas. Furthermore, investigation into management accounts, especially acreage limitations, would have pitted some western states against others and further challenged the already shaky coalition supporting water projects.

Concluding Thoughts

Because the Bureau of Reclamation is an example of a classic pork-barrel agency, one would expect to see the strongest support for the self-interest model there. But the relationships between the BOR and the Interior committees diverge from the self-interest model and fit better with the policy model. Even in what can be considered a prototypical subgovernment, significant conflicts between the bureau and the committees emerged. The disputes centered on the direction of the reclamation program as bureaucrats and legislators advanced their own perspectives of desirable policy. Because the congressional committees were responsive to new issues and demands raised by other legislators, they blocked bureau policies that they probably would have supported in the past. The bureau had a well-defined, cohesive view of its mission and did not incorporate these new issues into its policies without legislative encouragement.

Disputes arose not from outsiders grabbing control of the agenda but because committee members paid attention to additional issues. In the early 1960s an ideological and partisan conflict blocked three bureau projects as committee members questioned the role of the federal government in producing and selling power. In the mid-1960s the Lower Colorado River Basin Project was held up first by an internal dispute among the reclamation states and then by a debate over the environmental consequences of the Bridge and Marble Canyon dams. Although outsiders were sometimes involved in these issues, they did not have to pressure the committees to address them, nor did they have to take control of the decision making. The committee members were attuned to these issues and were willing to address them.

Starting in the mid-1970s, the reclamation program was attacked more and more often as disputes no longer centered only on individual projects but on the entire scope of the reclamation program. Few new water projects were authorized. Stricter requirements on the method of financing were adopted, and appropriations for certain projects were difficult to obtain. Leaders had a more difficult time building and maintaining supportive coalitions. Vocal opponents of the reclamation program sat on the committees as well as in the chambers. When a bill finally made it out of a committee to be reported on the floor, its proponents could not assume that committee members would support the measure. The lack of unity meant that coalition leaders had to make concessions before the bill was reported out of the committee in order to fend off opponents. Lacking an effective strategy to build consensus, the BOR reluctantly accepted many of the changes in its program.

Conflict between the bureau and the committees did not fracture the subgovernment because conflict on one issue did not automatically lead to a dispute on another. The interactions between the bureau and the committees could move from conflict to consensus and back again. In the late 1970s and early 1980s, when the debate centered on the direction of the reclamation program, conflict became more frequent, but agreement could still be reached on some particular items as policy makers negotiated their differences.

Notes

1. *Congressional Record*, July 26, 1962, p. 14825.

2. The states are Arizona, California, Colorado, Idaho, Kansas, Montana, Nebraska, Nevada, New Mexico, North Dakota, Oklahoma, Oregon, South Dakota, Texas, Utah, Washington, and Wyoming.

3. Michael C. Robinson, *Water for the West*, p. 79.

4. The Hoover Dam was selected as one of seven civil engineering wonders in 1955 by the American Society of Civil Engineers. See William E. Warne, *The Bureau of Reclamation*, p. 37.

5. *Congress and the Nation*, vol. 1, p. 808.

6. Ibid., p. 81.

7. Ibid., p. 1766.

8. *Congressional Quarterly Weekly Report*, October 20, 1961, p. 1766.

9. U.S. Congress, House Committee on the Interior, Subcommittee on Irrigation and Reclamation, *Hearings on the Burns Creek Project*, p. 34.

10. *Congressional Record*, July 13, 1962, p. 15094.

11. The Central Arizona Project (CAP) is the main part of the Lower Colorado River Basin Project. CAP could only be authorized as part of the Basin Project because of the legal claims to water. Many congressional references use the two names interchangeably. I use CAP to refer to the entire project for simplicity's sake.

12. Richard L. Berkman and W. Kip Viscusi, *Damming the West*, p. 116. An acre foot is the amount of water needed to cover one acre a foot deep.

13. A *reconnaissance* study is a very quick, light study that does not require congressional authorization. A *feasibility* study is a thorough study of the possibility of constructing a project and requires congressional authorization.

14. The *New York Times*, July 22, 1966, p. 17.

15. Bureau administrators I spoke with said that even though the moratorium was over they would not even think about proposing an importation study.

16. Roderick Nash, *Wilderness and the American Mind*, p. 228.

17. *Congress and the Nation*, vol. 2, p. 533. Throughout the text I use "administration" to indicate the White House or the department.

18. The *New York Times*, July 28, 1966, p. 21 and June 15, 1966, p. 29.

19. *Congressional Quarterly Almanac, 1968*, p. 449.

20. Richard F. Fenno, Jr., *Congressmen in Committees*, pp. 58–59; and Morris P. Fiorina, *Congress: The Keystone of the Washington Establishment*, pp. 39–49.

21. For example, Representative Udall (D–AZ) interrupted the hearing on the San Felipe division with a tirade about CAP. Ignoring the reprimands of the chairman, Udall finished his harangue by saying, "I am serving notice that I think this bill ought to go forward only when our bill goes forward." U.S. Congress, House Committee on the Interior, Subcommittee on Irrigation and Reclamation, *Hearings on the San Felipe Division of the Central Valley Project, California*, p. 53.

22. Randall B. Ripley and Grace A. Franklin, *Congress, the Bureaucracy, and Public Policy*, pp. 111–113.

23. *Congressional Quarterly Almanac, 1981*, p. 1442.

24. Interview with staff member.

25. Interview with staff member.

26. Interview with BOR official.

27. Interview with staff member.

28. The Water Resources Program of the National Wildlife Federation, *Short-changing the Treasury*, May 22, 1984.

29. Interview with BOR official.

30. Interview with BOR official.

31. These roll-call votes were selected from the *Congressional Quarterly Almanac*. To be included, votes had to have a ten-percent dissent rate. The CQ polls and announcements were also coded.

32. Interview with staff member.

33. In 1986 cost sharing was adopted as part of the financing for all projects built by the Army Corps of Engineers. The provision would force local communities and users to pay about twenty-five percent of the cost of new projects. An agreement on cost sharing broke the impasse that had prevented the adoption of an omnibus bill for ten years. *Congressional Quarterly Weekly Report*, March 29, 1986, pp. 713–715.

34. Interview with staff member.

35. *Congressional Quarterly Weekly Report*, October 27, 1984, p. 2798.

36. Interview with staff member.

37. Interview with staff member.

38. Interview with staff member.

39. *Congressional Quarterly Weekly Report*, May 5, 1984, p. 1009.

40. Fenno, *Congressmen in Committees*, p. 5.

41. Reflecting this, the Senate Interior Committee changed its name to the Senate Energy and Natural Resources Committee in 1977.

42. Metzenbaum does not always have the votes to win in committee. His strategy is to put a legislative hold on the bills and refuse to agree to a time limit for the debate. Before they come up for a floor vote, the leadership consults with him about the bills, and he tries to win concessions. Interview with staff member.

43. Interview with ex-staff member.

44. Ibid.

45. Ibid.

46. Interview with BOR official.

47. Interview with BOR official.

48. Ibid.

49. R. Douglas Arnold, *Congress and the Bureaucracy*, p. 51.

50. Ibid., pp. 44–46.

51. Aaron Wildavsky, *The Politics of the Budgetary Process*, pp. 74–84.

52. This was true even for agencies like the Food and Drug Administration and the Bureau of Indian Affairs.

53. This situation may soon change. Representative George Miller (D–CA), who replaced Representative Udall (D–AZ) as the chair of the House Interior Committee in 1991, is a vocal critic of the Bureau of Reclamation. "You wouldn't hire the Bureau of Reclamation to build you a doghouse," he said in 1985. "Every one of their projects has massive cost overruns. Every one has massive environmental insults; every one is basically publicly unacceptable." *Congressional Quarterly Weekly Report*, January 25, 1986, pp. 161–163.

54. Available evidence about the management of the bureau suggests that investigations would uncover incidents in which the bureau has managed accounts so as to unduly minimize costs to water users. The Water Resources Program of the National Wildlife Federation, *Shortchanging the Treasury*, May 22, 1984.

3

The Bureau of Indian Affairs

Red, no, I mean white tape.
—Buffey St. Marie, *Ms.*, March 1975

The Bureau of Indian Affairs (BIA) administers a broad variety of programs that cut across a number of functional areas. The primary agency that executes the federal government's responsibilities to Indians* living on reservations, it handles such matters as education, welfare programs, law enforcement, and the protection of natural resources. Although many other agencies provide similar services to American Indian tribes, the bureau is unique because it has authority over the trust responsibility. The trust responsibility refers to the federal government's obligation to guard and protect the land and resources of the tribes. Under this responsibility, the BIA works with tribes as governing bodies of reservations.

It is difficult to categorize the bureau according to the typology underlying the subgovernment model. Some of its programs, such as building roads and school buildings, would be distributive policy; other responsibilities such as welfare programs would be redistributive. Because its constituency is an easily identified and concentrated group and the opposition is not well organized, it probably fits best with distributive policy. This decision is also consistent with earlier research. From J. Leiper Freeman's work we know that a subgovernment dominated the decision making in Indian affairs during the 1950s.[1]

---

*Throughout this book I use the term "Indians" to refer to Native Americans. Because the bureau that provides services to tribes is named the Bureau of Indian Affairs and policy makers refer to "Indian affairs policy," I continued to use the term "Indians" for consistency.

One might expect, then, consensus policy making guided by a traditional subgovernment. From 1961 to 1984 the Bureau of Indian Affairs certainly operated within a subgovernment. The dominant policy makers were the congressional committees, the agency, and a number of interest groups. Issues were not framed in partisan terms, and they were seldom addressed by the House or Senate chamber. As illustrated by Table 3.1, few roll-call votes were taken in either the House or the Senate. Occasionally a president requested that a new policy be devised, but no administration placed a high priority on any policy initiative.

The dominance of a subgovernment, however, did not lead to the dominance of consensus and the relative absence of conflict. Freeman was correct when he identified the conflict that pervaded this policy area in the 1950s.[2] In the next two and a half decades, 1961 to 1984, conflict continued to emerge between the bureau and its authorizing committees, the House and Senate Interior committees.[3] It is not sufficient, however, to merely point out that conflict existed. This chapter elaborates on the rise and fall of conflict and consensus, relying on the policy model to explain when and why conflict emerged.

The pattern of conflict between the BIA and the committees does not fit with the self-interest model, but the policy model helps us to understand the actions of both the committees and the bureau, actions that otherwise seem inexplicable. Conflict rose and fell as both the committees and the bureau advanced their own perspective of appropriate public policy. Committee members were very concerned with the administrative capabilities of the bureau, and they tried to ensure that the implementation of policies was consistent with their own policy views. Despite the intensity of conflict, disputes did not break down the subgovernment. Even conflict over fundamental policy issues did not structure the debate on other policy questions.

Conflicts over Major Policy Directions

The major conflicts between the agency and the committees centered around the mission of the agency. Until the mid-1970s the two groups could not agree on a major, overarching Indian policy. The bureau had to defend its programs from attacks by legislators who wished to restrict the role of the agency. Questions of major policy directions were extremely difficult to resolve because of disagree-

Table 3.1

Number of Roll-Call Votes on Indian Affairs Issues in the House and Senate, 1961 to 1984

Year	House	Senate
1961	0	1
1962	0	0
1963	0	0
1964	0	1
1965	0	0
1966	0	0
1967	0	0
1968	0	0
1969	1	0
1970	0	6
1971	2	0
1972	0	0
1973	1	0
1974	4	1
1975	2	1
1976	1	0
1977	2	0
1978	10	0
1979	2	0
1980	2	0
1981	0	0
1982	3	1
1983	1	0
1984	0	0

Source: Roll-call votes were collected from the *Congressional Quarterly Almanac,* volumes dated from 1961 to 1984. Votes needed a ten-percent dissent rate, the standard rate for roll-call analysis, to be counted.

ment about the solutions as well as the problems.

Before a consensual solution was reached in the 1970s, two major disputes developed between the committees and the agency as each group presented distinct policy aims. The bureau wanted to protect its trust responsibility, and it opposed any policies that limited the agency's responsibility for guarding the land and resources of the tribes. The committees believed that the bureau was too paternalistic; they searched for a policy that gave greater independence to the Indians living on reservations. Consensus finally emerged when a solution was discovered that could meet both of these policy views.

The Policy of Termination

Until around 1967, the Bureau of Indian Affairs and the Interior committees clashed over the fundamental direction and nature of Indian
policy. Both committees, and especially the Senate Interior Committee,
supported the policy of termination that had been expressed by Congress in a resolution adopted in 1953.[4] Termination meant that reservations would be disbanded, and tribal assets would be distributed among
individual members. To the extent that tribes would be governing
units, they would be like local governments subject to state laws. Termination was a tremendous shift in the federal government's relationships with Indians because it would have ended the trust responsibility;
tribes would no longer be served by the federal government, and their
natural resources would not be protected by the federal government.

Immediately after the resolution was passed, four tribes were sin-
gled out for congressional action. Between 1954 and 1959, ten more
termination acts were passed.[5] The wave of acts then subsided, but the
Interior committees in the early 1960s were still trying to terminate
services to several tribes. Faced with a policy that would eventually
eliminate the agency and the trust responsibility, the bureau did what it
could to oppose termination. Gradually, support for termination, as
well as the conflict that surrounded it, declined throughout the 1960s.
Although the policy was not officially altered until 1973, neither committee pursued it after 1966, and the debate over the essential aspects
of Indian policy subsided.

The philosophy behind termination emerged from both a general
ideological view of government and concern over this particular policy
area. The policy was part of a larger effort by the conservative Republican majority in Congress and President Eisenhower in the 1950s to
reduce the size and role of the government. But it also stemmed from a
basic dislike of the unique treatment received by Indians on reservations and the supposed incompetence of the bureau. It was these elements of the philosophy that contributed to the continued support for
termination after the Republican majority gave way to a liberal Democratic majority favoring an expanded role for the federal government.[6]

Termination was an attack on the bureau as well as on the Indian
tribes. Members criticized the agency's failure to raise the standard of
living on the reservations and were suspicious of the large bureaucracy
involved in the daily lives of Indians. A common accusation was that

the main concerns of bureau personnel were to get promoted and to perpetuate the bureaucracy.[7] For example, Senator Henry Dworshak (R–ID) claimed that Indians were starving on their reservations and that the only solution was to get rid of the Bureau of Indian Affairs.[8] Representative E.Y. Berry (R–SD) charged that the bureau's program was the "most vicious of any Socialist system in the world" and that reservations were "sanctuaries for bureaucracy in its most complete and devastating form."[9]

The issue was one of maintaining the agency, not extending its scope, and the attacks forced the agency to defend and justify its mission. Because both the Eisenhower and the Kennedy administrations officially supported termination, public opposition by the bureau was restrained. However, both commissioners in these administrations tried to protect the tribes under attack. Clashes between Commissioner Phileo Nash and Senator Henry Jackson (D–WA), the chairman of the Senate Interior Committee, over the termination of the Colville tribes have been cited as one reason for Nash's dismissal.[10] After Nash was forced to resign in 1966, Commissioner Robert Bennett continued to resist termination and helped the Seneca Indians to fight it by encouraging them to seek the assistance of their congressional delegation.[11]

Unfortunately for the agency, there were few tactics it could use to fight termination. The strategy of the agency was to drag its feet to slow termination and to write legislative proposals that were less harsh than those drafted by termination supporters. For example, in the Colville legislation, the bureau devised a plan that would continue a part of the reservation for those Indians who did not want to be terminated. Although procrastination was a strategy of last resort, it was also somewhat effective because the committees delegated the task of drafting termination plans to the agency.

This strategy helped to slow termination, but it did not build support for the bureau. The committees reacted by chastising the agency for moving so slowly; they had the perfect opportunity to complain that the bureau wanted to manage the tribes only so it could maintain itself. The Senate Interior Committee told the bureau to relinquish its control over the Indians, asserting that the bureau "had tenaciously held onto its wards, without whom it would have no reason to exist."[12] Despite the official support of termination, not all committee members supported it. Their opposition prevented the termination of some tribes. For example, Representative James Haley (D–FL), a member of the House Interior

Committee, repeatedly blocked termination of the Colville tribe by not letting the bill out of committee after the Senate committee repeatedly passed the measure at Senator Jackson's urging.[13]

Termination policy withered away slowly in the late 1960s and early 1970s. The policy was abandoned as committee members realized it was not very effective. The desertion of the policy was probably due more to opposition from other groups than the efforts of the agency.[14] Indian tribes and associations such as the National Congress of American Indians fiercely protested the policy. Reports on those tribes that had been terminated highlighted the difficulties and problems confronting the tribes. State and local governments found they were overwhelmed by the need to provide services for American Indians.

With these reports, enthusiasm for termination waned, and Indian affairs drifted until the Nixon Administration's push to create a new policy in 1973. Even though the committees stopped promoting termination in 1967, neither committee tried to replace it with some other approach to guide the federal government's relationships with the tribes. Rather it was the agency that attempted to set a new direction for Indian policy. In the second dispute over major policy directions, the agency's proposal for broad legislative changes was rejected by the congressional committees in 1966 and 1967.

The discord over this proposal followed from different perspectives on the bureau's intentions. To the bureau, the program was not only a much needed replacement for termination, it was also consistent with the domestic policy of the time—President Johnson's Great Society program. To the committees, the plan was merely another example of the bureau's paternalistic attitude toward American Indians. The opposition of the tribes confirmed the legislators' conclusion. Unable to alter the committees' attitude toward the agency, the bureau could not create a supporting coalition for the program, and no legislation was enacted.

The bureau moved to alter its fundamental policies in 1966 and 1967 in response to the Johnson Administration's request to raise the economic position of American Indians. President Johnson wanted the most comprehensive, far-sighted, and adventuresome program to help Indians in the nation's history.[15] Commissioner Bennett called the legislation "the first major milestone" in government–Indian relations since the 1934 Indian Reorganization Act.[16] Labeled the Indian Resource Development Act of 1967, the proposal was designed to facilitate the attainment of loans and grants for business development on reservations.[17]

Although the Resource Development Act was supposed to be major legislation that would herald a new era in Indian affairs, the congressional committees reacted with little enthusiasm. The bill was introduced in Congress in 1967 at the request of the Johnson Administration, not because there was support for its provisions.[18] The consensus among departmental witnesses before both the House and the Senate subcommittees was that the members were not impressed by the legislation and did not see it as a great landmark.[19] The same criticisms that were directed at the bureau in reference to termination surfaced in the congressional hearings. Members felt the bureau was too interested in maintaining control over Indians' affairs and continuing the paternalism that many felt pervaded the government's Indian policy:

[Rep. John Saylor (R–PA):] My reading of this bill as it stands right now reminds me of saying to the Indians that you are going to give him a horse, a blanket, and a job, but you put a noose around his neck when you give it to him. The noose is in the hands of the Secretary. If you do not ride the horse the way the Secretary likes it, if you do not wrap yourself in the blanket the way the Secretary likes it, the Secretary is going to yank that rope and pull you right down off the horse.[20]

Despite the fact that there was no overarching policy in Indian affairs, no legislative entrepreneur rose to grab the opportunity to rework the bill into a more satisfying and comprehensive measure. Hearings were held, and the matter was dropped.

The bureau was not able to combat this congressional indifference through interest-group enthusiasm. The bureau's proposal floundered when it did not get the endorsement of its constituents. Indian tribes were opposed to the bill partly because of fears of termination; support for that approach was still emanating from the congressional committees. Only a year earlier, the Senate Interior Committee held up Bennett's nomination as commissioner while it wrote a report chastising the bureau for not implementing termination policy. During hearings on the resource development bill, Aspinall asked the Secretary of the Interior if this legislation supported "termination and the emancipation of the American Indian." His words left little doubt as to what he felt the Secretary's response should be:

> Do you see this legislation as pointing toward possible termination of wardship at the discretion and the choice of the Indians themselves, or is this just one more statement that we make to try to make everybody believe that the Indians are coming into their rightful place in all of our activities?[21]

The agency's attempts to mitigate the opposition and create a supportive coalition failed. Both the bureau and the department tried to persuade Indians that the proposals did not mean termination, and they tried to include Indians in the development of the provisions. Initially, this started out well. In 1966 Commissioner Bennett held a series of meetings with Indians across the country to receive their suggestions. Unfortunately, the department's preliminary draft of the legislation was made public before the discussions and negotiations with the Indians were completed. Faced with what they saw as evidence of the bureau's insincerity and duplicity and believing that their participation was merely cooptation, American Indians furiously opposed the legislation. Without any support from the supposed beneficiaries of the bill, committee members had little reason to act on the legislation.

The Policy of Self-Determination

The new direction for Indian affairs finally came with the Nixon Administration, and it brought a period of relative consensus between the committees and the bureau. This consensus arose because the committees and the bureau found a policy, called self-determination, that fit their disparate views. Under this policy, designed to reduce paternalism, Indian tribes were supposed to have the opportunity to administer their own programs. Self-determination meant that the bureau's responsibilities would change from administration and oversight of programs to grant-writing and technical assistance. Although critics took out the "d" and the "e" to read self-termination, the new policy was supposed to continue federal support and, at the same time, bring a modern era of Indian control over their own programs.[22]

Under the umbrella of the new, overarching policy of self-determination, a spate of bills was acted on by the committees in 1973 and 1974. Land around Blue Lake, New Mexico, was returned to the Pueblo Indians. Federal recognition was returned to the Menominee tribe, officially ending the policy of termination. Economic development loans and grants were authorized. The Alaskan Natives Settlement Act was passed.[23]

Self-determination received support from legislators because it granted more authority to the tribes. It did not suffer from the paternalism that legislators felt plagued earlier policies. Despite the fact that this meant a reduced role for the agency, the bureau endorsed the proposal. Self-determination was designed to enhance the independence and economic status of the tribes without forcing cultural assimilation. More important, it would accomplish this goal without sacrificing the trust responsibility. The federal government retained its responsibility to protect the land and natural resources of the tribes.

The consensus that developed at this time is consistent with the policy model but not with the self-interest model. Only the assumptions of the policy model lead to the expectation that an agency would support a restricted role for its programs. Because budget-maximizing bureaucrats would oppose automatically any proposal that reduced their authority and thus their budget, the self-interest model predicts conflict in this situation. The critical role played by several key legislators in passing self-determination is also consistent with the policy model. Legislators in both the House and the Senate used their leadership positions in the committees to shift the direction of Indian affairs.

Although consensus prevailed during this period, self-determination aroused some hostility among both bureaucrats and legislators. An implicit aim of self-determination was reducing the bureaucracy, because its logical end was that tribes would administer all of their own programs with little need for a central agency. Not unpredictably, there was some antagonism from bureau employees as they recognized these implications. Opposition came primarily from the area offices, the individuals most directly involved in running the daily affairs of Indian programs and those whose jobs were most likely to be threatened. The congressional tendency to stress the number of jobs that could be cut through self-determination did nothing to alleviate these fears.[24]

The reaction of these career civil servants stemmed from more than a simple concern about losing jobs. The bureaucrats were confused about the attacks on their authority. They did not understand why their expertise was questioned:

> We knew what was best, we were the experts, we knew who to hire—the teachers, the social workers. We were the keepers of the knowledge.

It was not easy for us to say, you mean, we've been running the program all this time and next year these guys with no experience are going to run it?[25]

These civil servants felt they were being undercut, that for years they had been proclaimed the experts and now they were denied that status. They were trying to protect the authority of the agency. Their opposition is understandable in the context of the policy model; they believed they were the experts who should be granted discretion in administering the programs.

The status of the agency was threatened by self-determination, as it was in the termination era, but dominant parts of the bureau still upheld the policy. Bureau officials worked enthusiastically with White House advisers to frame the new proposal. In fact, the BIA tried to promote self-determination before Congress acted on the Nixon Administration's proposal. The agency used some early laws, such as the Buy-Indian Act of 1916, to justify contracting programs out to the tribes.[26] Bureaucrats in the Washington office saw their chance for a forceful push to protect Indian rights and fulfill the government's obligation to Indians that had been neglected for years. The leading advocates were Commissioners Louis Bruce and Morris Thompson as well as a number of young activist civil servants called "the young Turks."[27]

Just as a few key administrators were central to the support from the bureau, committee leaders endorsed the policy of self-determination and persuaded committee members to follow them. These legislators, the preference outliers of the policy model, identified the new policy as one they wanted to pursue. In 1974 two new chairmen of the subcommittees on Indian affairs, Senator James Abourezk (D–SD) and Representative Lloyd Meeds (D–WA), were leading proponents of the policy. Crucial support from the chairman of the Senate Interior Committee, Henry Jackson (D–WA), emerged from his hopes of a presidential nomination. Jackson's aides saw his fight to terminate the Colville tribe as a black spot on a good record on domestic policy, one that could be used against him in the race for the presidency. They persuaded him to revamp his positions on Indian affairs.[28]

These committee leaders were able to convince both the Democratic and the Republican members to support the policy changes. The Democratic leadership was assisted in its endeavors by the Nixon Administration's involvement in a traditionally Democratic issue.

Nixon's message about Indian policy in 1970 highlighted the need to take immediate action to protect and advance the rights and culture of a minority group, an aim that was usually considered the province of the Democratic party.[29] Democrats could not very well allow the Republicans to move in on one of their specialties. The Republican minority, at least on the Senate Interior Committee, "wasn't too pleased with the message because it went against their ingrained, western philosophy—how in hell do we get at these resources?"[30] But they eventually sided with their Republican president to provide a bipartisan coalition in support of the legislation.

These disputes over major policy directions as well as the consensus surrounding self-determination fit with the policy model but not the self-interest model. First, the committees and the agency had different views of desirable public policy in Indian affairs, and each pressed forward with its own perspective. Not until a policy was discovered that satisfied these divergent views did consensus develop.

Second, some of the interactions make sense only in the context of the policy model. The bureau's support of self-determination, a policy that reduced the role of the agency, is consistent only with the assumption that an agency pursues policy goals. The self-interest model predicts conflict in this case because budget-maximizing bureaucrats would oppose reductions in their authority that could lead to budget cuts.

Third, conflict was not raised by outsiders, but by the interactions of the committees and the bureau. It was the committee members who pressed forward with termination, and the committee members who refused to support the bureau's resource development plan. Outsiders displayed little interest in Indian affairs; even Presidents Johnson and Nixon did not place a high priority on passage of legislation when they requested new initiatives.

Strategies to Obtain Consensus

Despite these conflicts over fundamental directions in Indian affairs, consensus was maintained on a number of other issues. The conflict over major policy issues did not spill over to other interactions. The bureau and the committees agreed on a variety of issues even when they could not agree on the overarching policy for the agency. As the policy model predicts, the system was loosely coupled rather than tightly woven. Because issues were differentiated, conflict was not disruptive and did not force the subgovernment to adapt or disintegrate.

Consensus arose in a variety of ways. First, consensus was maintained by disaggregating issues so that they could be handled on a case-by-case basis. Second, consensus emerged when an issue could be framed to fit whatever overarching policy was fashionable. The bureau's education programs escaped some of the attacks visited on the agency because they fit with termination, economic development, and self-determination. Finally, accord developed because the bureau as well as the committees accepted a restricted jurisdiction for the agency; the bureau did not push for an expanded jurisdiction even when it had the opportunity to do so.

At first glance, the extent of consensus on Indian affairs issues seemed overwhelming. Committees were not partisan, bills were generally passed on the floor by unanimous consent, many bills had the support of all parties involved, and a large number of bills were passed each session. One staff member became very upset at the suggestion that certain conflictual issues were avoided by the legislators:

> All you have to do is look at the record, the reports of the committees, look at what we've done. From 1970 to 1980, 607 of the 4723 bills referred to this committee, that's thirteen percent, were Indian affairs. Of the bills reported, twenty-six percent were Indian affairs. Of the bills signed into law, thirty percent were Indian affairs. I fail to see, just on those numbers alone, how that could be.[31]

The supposed consensus, however, is somewhat misleading. Decision makers found it difficult to construct overarching policy because of the considerable conflict on major issues. To prevent disputes from blocking progress on all issues, strife was avoided by disaggregating them. This tactic meant that conflict did not immobilize decision making, but it was not a very successful strategy for helping to create support for the BIA.

Consensus agreements could not be reached easily on broad policy issues, but they could usually be hammered out on a specific issue that affected a particular reservation. By disaggregating the issues and dealing with them on a case-by-case basis, members from other areas did not care as much about the problem and would acquiesce to the proposed solution:

> If we have a problem, it is a lot easier to narrow the solution so that it only deals with one case. Then the others say that doesn't affect us so it's all right, and we can address the problem. If we deal with things across the board, each situation is a little different, and then we have to deal with a lot more senators, too.... So if we can't get something

through, we'll narrow it and limit it. Very few senators want to get involved in a problem for another state.[32]

This suggests an emphasis on local benefits rather than general benefits.[33] The advantages of this strategy were that conflict was avoided, an aura of consensus and cooperation was maintained, and a few problems in a few tribes were resolved. It probably also allowed members to balance more easily the contradictory demands of non-Indians and Indians that developed on many questions of governing reservations. However, many issues were not considered, and only a few tribes had the resources for the sophisticated political activity that yielded a response. Also, some types of problems were never really addressed because broad policy questions were avoided.

Second, consensus developed when a policy could fit whatever overarching policy happened to be dominant. The education programs were able to sustain congressional support even when there was criticism of the bureau and a desire to reduce federal involvement in Indian affairs. These included vocational education, primary and secondary schools, and tribally controlled community colleges. The advantage of these programs was that they could be viewed in different ways by those with different ideologies. They could be perceived as ways to achieve the financial independence of Indians, assimilate them into mainstream white society, and eventually remove the need for governmental protection. Thus, they could survive in periods when conservatives who wished to eliminate reservations and the unique position of Indians dominated policy making. But it was also relatively easy to make minor changes in the programs, such as promoting Indian control over education, to please more liberal perspectives.

Even in 1956, during the period of termination, an Indian vocational education training act was adopted, and the authorization level was increased three times in the 1960s. Initially, vocational education was coupled with a relocation program that helped to move Indians off the reservation. As termination ended, the relocation program was dropped, but assistance for vocational education continued. At a time when they were vigorously attacking the BIA, legislators praised vocational education as one of the most successful programs in Indian affairs and cited the waiting list for entrance into the program as evidence of support from the Indian community.

Similarly, aid to primary and secondary education was continued throughout the years of this study, and aid for postsecondary schools was authorized in the 1970s. The bureau's policy in the 1950s and 1960s of moving Indian children to public schools as often as possible yielded to a greater emphasis on involving Indians in the governing of their schools when the focus shifted to self-determination. In the early 1970s, aid to tribally controlled community colleges developed first by assisting a school run by the Navajos and then spread to a general program to help other tribes to establish similar schools. During the Reagan Administration, a time of program cuts and retrenchment, the Senate committee extended the trust authority to education and in oversight hearings focused on preventing proposed cuts in the bureau's educational programs.[34]

The support of these programs by legislators does not mean that the bureau was immune to criticisms in education. Despite their support for the educational programs, legislators were not willing to give the agency free rein. Oversight hearings were held frequently to examine bureau decisions in education. In the 1980s, much attention was concentrated on the bureau's move to close some boarding schools, and the agency was chastised for not having the facts to justify its decision.[35] Staff members often mentioned this as a major concern among members. However, congressional approval of educational programs continued even when members were disgruntled with the agency.

Because these educational programs could be viewed in a variety of ways, they were upheld by those with different views of the role of government and could survive periods when there was little support for an active and aggressive Bureau of Indian Affairs:

> [Sen. William Cohen (R–ME):] You can get by somewhat even if they cut back on food. You can get by without adequate housing, but if you cut out education, then you have nothing because you have no hope for the future.[36]

The underlying belief in equal opportunity, a prominent value in American society,[37] sustained the education programs. Other programs could be neglected or abolished, but education could still solve problems.

Finally, the Bureau of Indian Affairs reduced conflict and increased consensus when it refrained from pushing for an extended role for the agency. The bureau had two opportunities to press for a major expansion of its services, once in the 1960s and again in the early 1970s. Guided by a view of the agency's mission, the bureau's leaders did not try to acquire new responsibilities. At both times the committees were not very supportive of BIA programs; the agency's inaction averted a fight over expanding the bureau's tasks.

In the 1960s, dramatic changes in Indian affairs occurred outside of the agency, as both Presidents Kennedy and Johnson emphasized economic development on reservations.[38] As part of the Great Society's war on poverty, individual Indians and tribes became eligible for social service programs operated by other agencies. Almost any grant or loan provided to states and local governments was also provided to tribes. They began to receive funds for housing programs and public works projects. Funds for education were allocated to tribes through Headstart and the Elementary and Secondary Education Act. By 1970 the BIA controlled only fifty percent of federal funding for Indians.[39]

The leadership of the bureau pushed for this extension of services by the other agencies; they did not include the BIA in the competition for these responsibilities.[40] Some of the existing programs of the bureau, like the revolving loan fund, were expanded, but the type of services the bureau provided did not change. The agency did not jealously guard its position as the primary provider of goods and services to Indian tribes.

The BIA could afford to allow other agencies to provide services to Indians on reservations because the others' involvement did not jeopardize the need for the agency. The Economic Development Administration could construct public works projects. The Department of Housing and Urban Development could improve the quality of the housing stock. The Department of Transportation could build roads, providing better access to a number of reservations. By endorsing the inclusion of Indian tribes as grant recipients, the BIA knew that more resources would go to the tribes. Yet the agency also knew that its central mission, the trust responsibility, would not be touched by these changes. The agency would still have a unique responsibility, one that other agencies would find it almost impossible to acquire.

A push by the bureau to remain the primary conduit for funds and programs on the reservations would have sparked vehement discussions in the Interior committees. The committees, still tied up with termination, were aggravated with the bureau's supposed inadequacy, paternalism, and selfishness. Charges that the agency wanted to protect and enlarge itself rather than serve the Indians probably would have risen. This debate was avoided because the new responsibilities were given to other agencies. The authorizing committees that dealt with the proposals, such as the House Education and Labor and the Senate Labor and Welfare committees, were not involved in the dispute over termination. They could authorize legislation to provide additional resources to the tribes without having to consider the ability of the BIA to administer the programs.

The second opportunity the bureau had to expand was in the mid-1970s. The act authorizing the programs of the BIA, the Snyder Act, says that the agency can provide services to Indians living on or near reservations. Traditionally, the agency interpreted this to mean that it would provide services only to Indians on reservations, with a few exceptions such as the Oklahoma Indians. Once an American Indian left the reservation, the responsibility of the bureau ended. The question that arose in the 1970s was whether the bureau should provide services to individual Indians, regardless of where they lived, or whether the agency should limit its jurisdiction to reservations. The agency chose to restrict its jurisdiction.

For many years the bureau's decision did not matter very much. Most American Indians lived on reservations. But in the second half of the twentieth century, American Indians began leaving the reservations and moving to cities such as Minneapolis, Denver, and Los Angeles. During the era of termination, the bureau encouraged Indians to move off the reservations through a relocation program. The bureau's decision to limit its jurisdiction meant that it did not serve a great number of American Indians. By 1980, the BIA provided services to only fifty-three percent of those persons identifying themselves as Indians.[41]

By the early 1970s, Indians who did not live on reservations, commonly referred to as urban Indians, were starting to become politically active in such organizations as the American Indian Movement. They established urban community service programs, helping Indians who had moved from the reservations. They organized protest marches, demanding that land be returned to Indian tribes. They insisted that religious practices should be exempt from federal laws. As a result of their political activities, policy makers started to wonder if the BIA's restricted jurisdiction was obsolete.

Some legislators and bureaucrats grumbled about extending services to urban Indians, and a few debates focused on whether current laws restricted the agency from expanding its jurisdiction. In 1972, fifty-eight members of Congress pressed Interior Secretary Rogers Morton to extend BIA services.[42] Representative Meeds expressed great concern in hearings to establish the American Indian Policy Review Commission that the interests of off-reservation Indians would be ignored by this study.[43] The American Indian Policy Review Commission concluded that the Snyder Act, the original act creating the bureau, had been interpreted too conservatively by the agency and that it was meant to cover all Indians, whether they lived on or off the reservations. The commission suggested a legislative mandate to recognize off-reservation Indians and their needs by both the Bureau of Indian Affairs and the Indian Health Service.[44]

Little action or even policy suggestions, however, came from these murmurings. The bureau did not attempt to provide services to urban Indians. It retained the notion that its relationship with Indians is from one government to another, not from one government to an individual, and that the federal government's trust responsibility covered natural resources but not individuals. The idea that programs could be extended to individual Indians became prominent in other social service agencies and enabled them to single out Indians as a disadvantaged group, like other minorities, that needed special assistance.[45]

The bureau was too constrained by its philosophy, its constituents, and its administration to press for an expansion of its jurisdiction. Indians who lived on reservations opposed such a change because they feared that funds would not be increased to cover the additional demand for services, and they would have to share what they currently received with additional individuals.[46] The bureau tended to share the viewpoint of its constituents, the Indians on the reservations. In addition, the agency's notion of the trust responsibility was too imbedded in the agency's mission for it to change easily. The agency was responsible not just for individuals but also for land and natural resources. Its mission was tied to the reservations, not to individual Indians. A bureau official asked about servicing individual Indians often replied, "that is not our mandate from Congress," with little consideration that maybe the mandate could have been changed.[47] At least as the employees defined the purpose and policies of the bureau, altering the agency's jurisdiction was a step that would significantly change the agency. One thoughtful bureau official observed that:

> If the bureau had to provide services to one million plus people instead of the current one-half million, we would be getting close to the end of

the bureau and maybe to the end of the reservations. We would never get that kind of money, and it would destroy the government-to-government relationship. The Indians have a much stronger claim to services than other groups. The courts ruled that special treatment for Indians isn't discrimination because it is based on these rights. The whole basis of the thing would crumble if someone went to court and argued that the situation has changed, and it isn't a government-to-government relationship anymore.[48]

The agency's reluctance to push for expansion of its services at these times had long-lasting effects because it reduced the likelihood that the agency would acquire additional responsibilities in the future. The lines of the bureau's authority became established and distinguished from those of the other agencies serving American Indians. When the Reagan Administration outlined proposals to eliminate the Department of Education, a transfer of the education programs to the BIA was opposed by the committees because the eligibility of off-reservation Indians would be curtailed.[49] The same response came when the White House suggested moving the social programs of the Administration for Native Americans from the Department of Health and Human Services to the BIA.[50]

The Rise of New Issues

In the late 1970s, a perplexing and complicated question, and one that most participants wished would disappear, demanded attention. This important development, one that continued into the 1980s, was the debate over tribal sovereignty and treaty rights. The tribal sovereignty issues stemmed from the fact that Indian tribes are independent governing entities exempt from many state laws.[51] The debate encompassed a broad variety of issues, including water rights, gambling, law enforcement, and fishing and hunting rights. These issues resulted in claims by non-Indians that Indians received special privileges not granted to other American citizens. The Indians responded that they were merely exercising their rights provided by treaties with the United States.

Because the BIA avoided involvement in many of these cases, the conflicts were not directly between the committees and the bureau in the sense of formal action directed at the agency. Yet the agency was caught up in the conflict even though it tried to minimize the controversies. The actions taken by the agency did not boost the image of the

BIA in Congress. Its standing was tied to that of the tribes, and its attempts to appear evenhanded and reasonable only generated complaints of ineffectiveness by both sides.

In the mid-1970s, Indian tribes started pressing for their treaty rights more vigorously. Two important cases crystallized attention and heightened the discord between Indians and non-Indians. In the Maine lands case, eastern tribes refused to settle for monetary compensation, demanding instead the return of land to their ownership.[52] Not only did this question the title of most of the state of Maine, it also indicated a significant change from the traditional settlement of land claims through monetary damages and thereby raised more uncertainty about future claims. The other major case, *Boldt* v. *Washington*, threw the Northwest into an uproar. In this case the Supreme Court upheld a lower court ruling that Indians in Washington could catch all the salmon they wanted to on the reservation and were entitled to fifty percent of the fish caught elsewhere.[53] The case evoked complaints that Indians received undue special privileges and benefits.

These issues were particularly tricky for members of Congress in whose states and districts there were reservations because they tended to infuriate non-Indians, who resented the supposed special treatment and privileges that Indians received. The scarcity of many of the resources involved, such as water in the West, merely heightened the intensity of both sides' views. In addition, the growing militancy of the Indians in the early 1970s destroyed the sympathy toward Indians that tended to come from non-Indians:

> Judged as a whole, Indian militancy was more harmful than it was good. Indians were favored as a people's civil rights issue because of the guilt feelings of what our forefathers had done and because Indians were a downtrodden, suppressed group. When they became militant, they lost the sense of righteousness in which they were clothed, they lost that deprived image that they had earlier.[54]

The involvement and unhappiness of the non-Indians meant that legislators found themselves caught between the conflicting demands of the Indians and the whites. Committee members could not ignore one or the other because both were their constituents. The same respondent continued:

> Indians took over and tied up the land, then there was the Boldt decision. These things converged. They caused the members to at least give

pause to the reflection that Indian causes had lost some of their champions, some of their edge. Indians get their support from states with a large Indian population, and they would lose that support because of constituent pressure. A lot of the drive went out after that.[55]

Even legislators who were very supportive of and active in Indian affairs yielded to the intense demands of the non-Indians. Those who did not defer soon enough or often enough were remembered as those with serious election problems. Almost every respondent discussing these issues mentioned the problems of Representative Lloyd Meeds (D–WA), who almost lost his 1976 reelection bid. An incumbent since 1964, Meeds' near-loss was attributed to his refusal to act against the *Boldt* v. *Washington* decision.

The fallout from these cases first landed in the Ninety-fifth Congress, 1977–78, when a number of bills that would have repealed all treaties between the United States government and Indian tribes, dismissed water and land claims, and terminated the federal government's trust responsibility were introduced.[56] Even Representative Meeds introduced bills to extend states' jurisdiction over certain issues as they would apply to non-Indians and to reduce the likelihood of tribes suing over water rights.[57] The bills were largely symbolic. Both the House and the Senate committees shelved all of them; no one had really expected the committees to act on them. However, they indicated the intensity of the views that Indians should not receive special privileges and that Indians, too, have to compromise in these settlements.

Committee members became somewhat reluctant to devote their time and energy to promoting the causes of the tribes and often avoided involvement in Indian affairs policy. Shortly after Meeds' near-defeat, the House Interior Committee eliminated the Indian Affairs Subcommittee because no one wanted to chair it. A similar fate in the Senate was avoided when Abourezk (D–SD) pushed for the establishment of a temporary Indian affairs committee. Staff members claimed that these actions did not indicate an unwillingness to get involved in Indian affairs. They argued that legislators served on the Senate Indian Affairs Committee because of their interest in the issues. Then they acknowledged that membership did not count in the tally of the number of committees members could serve on, so members did not have to make a choice between this and some other committee.[58]

The treaty rights and tribal sovereignty issues did not emerge as direct conflicts between the bureau and the committees because the agency avoided a decisive role in the cases.[59] One bureau official was particularly disgruntled with the agency when he first started working in the Washington, D.C., office because the acting assistant director did not know the administration's policy on water rights and other trust status cases.[60] Although this particular employee was not content with leaving things to the White House and the secretary, many in the agency were willing to let others take control of these issues. For example, until a court ruling forced them to do otherwise, the agency did not become involved in land claims cases brought by tribes that were not federally recognized. "The two tribes [in Maine] took us to court and won. The court said the bureau can't get away with this. The law says the bureau is responsible for protecting the Indians. So we can't sit on the sidelines and say, 'look at these people and all their problems.' "[61] Because the tribes were not federally recognized, the bureau claimed it had no right or responsibility to get involved. This position was consistent with other bureau policies that restricted the jurisdiction of the agency, and it was also a way to avoid potentially conflictual cases.

When the bureau was forced to get involved in a case, it tended not to follow a hardline, pro-Indian stance, even though it was supposed to be an advocate for Indian interests. It was much more likely to act as a mediator for the two sides, trying to develop a solution that was reasonable enough to get everyone's approval:

> The key is to keep the issues from getting red and white, so to speak. [*Q.* What does the bureau do to do that?] We work out settlements. We try to get the realization on the Indian side that they have to be reasonable. A tribe in Washington is pressing for $400 or $500 million! Now they're talking $40 or $50 million and that may be possible. There is no way we or the congressmen could get the treasury to fork out that much. If they go too far, they'll lose in court and the Congress. . . . We try to get both sides to be realistic.[62]

Despite these attempts to be cautious and avoid involvement in particularly conflictual issues, the treaty rights and tribal sovereignty cases still harmed the bureau. Its effort to adopt a conciliatory stance led to criticisms from both sides of the issue and little support from either. The bureau was denounced by individual members for not protecting Indian interests enough or for advancing them too much.

In addition, the agency lost political support because the Indians did. The primary reason the agency had congressional support was not the bureau itself, its ability to manage programs or initiate policies, but the constituency group the bureau served. When asked if the agency had a base of support on the Hill, one bureau official said, "The Indians have a core of support and that is stronger than the bureau's. On the Hill, they distinguish between the bad BIA and the good Indians."[63] In the new issues that arose, there was not as much support for the Indians. Most legislators recognized that the Indians had some legitimate claims, but there was concern that those claims became unreasonable. The issues aroused the non-Indians and forced the members of Congress to respond to their demands. Also, the disapproval of the claims spilled over to affect other issues in Indian affairs:

> People don't mind too much if their tax dollars are going to drunken, lazy, no-good Indians and to AFDC mothers. But if they [the whites] own land on the reservation, and the tribe zones that land, they get livid. They get exercised about their tax dollars going for Indians who get special privileges. [*Q.* Do these positions affect other issues?] Surely, when they get angry, their anger spreads to tribal taxation, tribal jurisdiction, hunting and fishing rights, ricing [harvesting rice]. They get in touch with their congressman and say why are our tax dollars going for health and welfare programs when the Indians get all of these other things.[64]

The issues of tribal sovereignty and treaty rights are the crux of U.S. policy toward Indian tribes. Conflicts over these issues have the potential to be explosive, generating debates that cannot be resolved through negotiation or compromise, but only by the dominance of one side over another. Despite this, the issues did not split apart the subgovernment because conflict was diffused by the committees as well as the BIA. While the approaches adopted by the agency may have lessened the overt conflicts, they did little to help to build political support for the bureau.

Questions of Management

Throughout this 1961–84 period, the committees often attacked the bureau's management practices. As the policy model suggests, the committees maintained a watchful eye over the BIA's administration of its programs. At different times, the committees had regular means through which they could address management questions. Until 1973, the House Interior Committee held meetings with top personnel every two years to review policy. More recently, the committees held hearings every year to review the budget submitted by the administration. Since the advent of the Senate Select Committee on Indian Affairs, there have been more oversight hearings with opportunities for disgruntled Indians and non-Indians to vent their frustrations. Criticisms of the agency's management have occurred fairly frequently during this period.

Members' frustrations with Indian programs were due partly to the way in which they are authorized. Few programs have to have their authorizations renewed periodically. Most have a blanket authorization from the Snyder Act, the act outlining the federal government's responsibilities to the reservations, because it simply indicates that the BIA is to provide for the general support and civilization of Indians.[65] This freed members from having to address the issues when they did not want to, but it also eliminated an automatic review of programs.

Occasionally, members attempted to acquire more control over the programs, seeking out ways to reduce the discretion of the BIA. In the mid-1970s, the committees, under the initiative of Senator Abourezk, batted around the idea of altering the Snyder Act so that programs would have to be reauthorized periodically. A major problem with this proposal was that many reservations were established by treaties and are constitutionally entitled to federal government services. Also, most tribes would probably be adamantly opposed to such an idea because of the possibility that the reauthorization would not be passed by Congress. A more recent idea was to adopt a BIA Fiscal Accountability Act, pushed by Representative Morris Udall (D–AZ), which would establish greater control over the ways in which the bureau spent its money.

It would be easy to argue that these attacks on management were symbolic and were unlikely to be followed by any sanctions of the agency or attempts to effect change. Because other issues were highly controversial and risky, members could have focused their attention on management, knowing that non-Indians as well as Indians would not be offended. As long as the members did not threaten the existence of the agency, Indians could think that the attacks meant the legislators were actually addressing their concerns. Non-Indians could believe that the members were not too sympathetic to the demands of the tribes if they showed a willingness to jab at the agency.

Such explanations, however, do not seem valid. Members could easily have avoided any of these implementation issues, and the self-interest model suggests that they would. Because many of the programs did not have to be reauthorized, legislators were not forced to examine the programs in order to keep them operating. The members, though, looked for ways to increase their involvement through such mechanisms as the Fiscal Accountability Act. This interest in management is consistent with the policy model, as legislators try to ensure that agencies administer programs in ways consistent with congressional policy views.

In addition, attacks that could have been symbolic to the legislature were not necessarily symbolic to the bureau. Many bureau employees acknowledged that the agency erred and that these attacks were not frivolous. Bureau officials often mentioned the internal problems of the agency.[66] Frequent turnover of top personnel meant constant delays in action and uncertainty about policy directions. Hiring practices moved many persons into positions for which they were not trained. Regulations and procedures tended not to be classified or recorded, meaning that new employees did not know what their predecessors did in certain cases. One official claimed he was probably the only person in the agency who did not want to see the BIA Fiscal Accountability Act adopted because others agreed that maybe the agency was too flexible and should be "locked into place."

The idea of symbolic politics implies that attacks occur because they are relatively easy for members to make and that there is little concern about actually correcting a problem. The fact that these criticisms were believed to be justified by bureau employees suggests that members might actually have tried to facilitate change and questions the symbolic nature of the oversight. Criticisms could still have been easy for members to make, especially when compared to the other more intractable issues they could act on. But it seems that these attacks were not all symbolic, that members were attempting to effect change in the administration of BIA programs.

Concluding Thoughts

Conflict between the Bureau of Indian Affairs and the congressional committees occurred quite frequently during these twenty-four years.

Congressional action tended to spark these disputes as legislators tried to shift the mission of the agency and expressed their unhappiness with bureau programs. The agency was generally placed in a defensive position. In response to the frequent congressional criticism, it had to defend its mission and justify its implementation of programs. Consistent with the policy model, conflicts emerged because the committees and the BIA had different views of the agency's mission. They resolved the question of the agency's overarching policy only by finding an approach that suited both views.

Unlike the budget-maximizing agency of the self-interest model, the BIA did not adopt an expansionary approach to policy making. The agency's behavior fit more closely with the policy model. It did not lobby for new tasks even when it had the opportunity to do so. In response to its perceived mission, its constituency and its political standing, the agency developed a more constrained view of its responsibilities. Out of a belief that the policy would assist Indians, the agency even supported self-determination, a policy that meant the reduction of the authority and position of the bureau. This constrained perspective did not eliminate conflict with the congressional committees, but it meant that serious ruptures with the committees were avoided. A more aggressive agency would have raised issues that would have encountered intense opposition from Congress.

Even though these disputes centered on the overarching policy in Indian affairs, the conflicts did not fracture the subgovernment. Although outsiders were sometimes involved, their role was minimal. Conflicts were usually raised—and resolved—by legislators and administrative officials. Although conflict did not stall policy making on all issues, it did shape the ways in which problems were addressed. Legislators dealt with specific cases on particular reservations. The BIA accepted a curtailed jurisdiction and did not press for extended responsibilities. Programs such as education were altered slightly to fit the reigning philosophy in Indian policy.

Unfortunately for the agency, the tactics which lessened conflict enough so that action could proceed did not also build support for the BIA. The agency found it difficult to develop strategies that created a supportive coalition. Without that backing, the congressional criticism could not be stopped. The BIA, to the extent that it tried, was rather unsuccessful in developing legislative allies who were willing to grapple with broad, major policies. The bureau tried to redirect policy in 1967 at the urging of the administration, but it was too weak to succeed.

The frequent criticisms of the agency as well as the threats to the bureau because of termination and self-determination weakened the agency's ability to promote Indian interests aggressively and to withstand opposition. Recent concerns with sovereignty and treaty issues exacerbated this situation because the primary reason for support of the agency, sympathy for American Indians, was questioned. The problem was compounded by the fact that strategies to build support did not work very well for the agency. A focus on major policy questions, or a general benefit strategy, produced considerable conflict with congressional committees. Avoiding these questions and disaggregating the issues reduced conflict but yielded no way to change opinions and also induced complaints that the agency was not aggressively advocating Indian interests.

Unlike the Bureau of Reclamation, which could risk a fight with Congress, the Bureau of Indian Affairs did not have the resources, the support, or the history to survive such conflicts. To a certain extent, this enhanced the likelihood that the agency would comply, or at least attempt to comply, with congressional directives. For example, I cannot imagine any of the other agencies covered in this study agreeing to a plan like the BIA Fiscal Accountability Act that would significantly reduce their discretion in administering their programs. A more submissive agency, however, is also more impotent. Substantial policy innovations or aggressive leadership were unlikely to come from the BIA. This, of course, aggravated the situation in which the agency often found itself and led to more and louder complaints about the agency's inabilities and incompetence.

Notes

1. J. Leiper Freeman, *The Political Process: Executive Bureau–Legislative Committee Relations.*
2. Ibid.
3. The Senate Select Committee on Indian Affairs was created in 1977.
4. House Concurrent Resolution 108.
5. Raymond Butler, "The Bureau of Indian Affairs: Activities since 1945."
6. James Sundquist outlines this change in congressional majorities in *Politics and Policy: The Eisenhower, Kennedy, and Johnson Years*, pp. 385–429.
7. U.S. Congress, House Committee on the Interior, Subcommittee on Indian Affairs, *Hearings on Policies, Programs, and Activities of the Department of the Interior*, 87th Cong., 1st sess., 1961, pp. 22–27.

8. The *New York Times*, April 26, 1961, p. 34.

9. U.S. Congress, House Committee on the Interior, Subcommittee on Indian Affairs, *Hearings on Policies, Programs, and Activities of the Department of the Interior*, 88th Cong., 1st sess., 1963, pp. 182–183.

10. Margaret Connell Szasz, "Phileo Nash, 1961–1966," in Robert M. Kvasnicka and Herman J. Viola, *The Commissioners of Indian Affairs 1824–1977*, p. 320.

11. Ibid., p. 327.

12. The *New York Times*, April 10, 1966, p. 64.

13. Interview with ex-staff member and BIA official.

14. Interview with BIA official.

15. The *New York Times*, April 28, 1966, p. 60.

16. The *New York Times*, April 17, 1966, p. 81.

17. Alan Sorkin, *American Indians and Federal Aid*, p. 97.

18. Vine DeLoria, Jr., *Behind the Trail of Broken Treaties*, p. 32.

19. July 21, 1967, memo from Marvin Sonosky, General Counsel, to general counsel's clients, BIA archives.

20. U.S. Congress, House Committee on the Interior, Subcommittee on Indian Affairs, *Hearings on Indian Resource Development Act of 1967*, p. 55.

21. Ibid., p. 48.

22. To this date, self-determination continues to be the official federal policy.

23. Bills providing for an Indian Trust Council Authority and an assistant secretary of Indian affairs were not passed. Members were skeptical of the need for and the effectiveness of a trust authority, and neither committee passed the bill. Passage of the other bill was blocked by a controversial, nongermane amendment, and it was not introduced again. Since then, assistant secretaries for Indian affairs have been appointed by using an unfilled position. But this is not required by law and can be halted by any administration at any time.

24. U.S. Congress, Senate Committee on the Interior, *Hearings on the Realignment of the BIA Central Office*.

25. Interview with BIA official.

26. This move sparked a struggle in the agency between two camps, one side following Commissioner Louis Bruce and jumping ahead on self-determination, the other side following John Crow, a BIA administrator who opposed early implementation of self-determination. The details of this fight are outlined in Jack D. Forbes, *Native Americans and Nixon: Presidential Politics and Minority Self-Determination 1969–1972*.

27. Ibid., pp. 42–43.

28. Interview with ex-staff member and BIA official.

29. Ibid.

30. Ibid.

31. Interview with staff member.

32. Ibid.

33. R. Douglas Arnold, *Congress and the Bureaucracy*, pp. 38–39.

34. *Congressional Quarterly Almanac, 1982*, p. 50; and *Congressional Quarterly Weekly Report*, December 22, 1983, p. 178.

35. U.S. Congress, Senate Select Committee on Indian Affairs, *Hearings on Closing of Off-Reservation Boarding Schools*.

36. U.S. Congress, Senate Select Committee on Indian Affairs, *Oversight Hearings on Indian Education*, p. 57.

37. Anthony King, "Ideas, Institutions and the Policies of Governments: A Comparative Analysis," p. 420.

38. Kennedy's task force in 1961 urged the economic development of tribes' natural resources, and Johnson in a speech to tribal representatives said that "Indian welfare had been placed in the forefront of the attack on poverty." Szasz, "Phileo Nash, 1961–1966," pp. 315–319.

39. Theodore W. Taylor, *American Indian Policy*, p. 70.

40. Ibid., p. 317, and Warren Cohen and Philip Mause, "The Indian: The Forgotten American," pp. 1818–1858. This is also apparent from the agency's comments on proposed legislation, BIA archives.

41. Taylor, *American Indian Policy*, p. 4.

42. Forbes, *Native Americans and Nixon*, p. 67.

43. U.S. Congress, House Committee on the Interior, Subcommittee on Indian Affairs, *Hearings on Establishment of the American Indian Policy Review Commission*, pp. 51–55.

44. American Indian Policy Review Commission, Task Force 8: Urban and Rural Non-Reservation Indians, p. 9.

45. Interview with BIA official.

46. Ibid.

47. Interview with BIA official.

48. Interview with BIA official.

49. U.S. Congress, Senate Select Committee on Indian Affairs, *Oversight Hearings on Indian Education*, p. 275.

50. U.S. Congress, Senate Select Committee on Indian Affairs, *Hearings to Amend the Native American Programs Act of 1974*, p. 1.

51. The largest unresolved issue is that of law enforcement, where questions of jurisdiction have never been decided.

52. Taylor, *American Indian Policy*, pp. 26–32.

53. Ibid., p. 45.

54. Interview with member of Congress. This reaction is consistent with Michael Lipsky's argument in "Protest as a Political Resource," pp. 1144–1158.

55. Interview with member of Congress.

56. The *National Journal*, August 26, 1978, pp. 1353–1355.

57. Ibid., pp. 1353–54.

58. Interviews with staff members.

59. The Department of the Interior recommends legal action to the Department of Justice which then initiates the case. In major cases, the decision to pursue legal action as well as legislative settlements tends to be made by those above the BIA.

60. Interview with BIA official.

61. Interview with BIA official.

62. Ibid.

63. Ibid.

64. Interview with staff member.

65. Taylor, *American Indian Policy*, p. 66.

66. Interviews with BIA officials.

4

The Food and Drug Administration

"She should be thinking of higher things."
"Nothing could be higher than food," said Leah.
—Ivy Compton-Burnett,
The Mighty and the Fall

The Food and Drug Administration (FDA) has a broad mandate to regulate foods, drugs, medical devices, and cosmetics in order to protect consumers from harmful products. The 1906 Food and Drug Act and the 1938 Food, Drug, and Cosmetic Act provide the foundation of the FDA's powers. Both acts were adopted shortly after investigative journalists revealed hazardous and unsanitary practices in the production and sale of drugs and foods.[1]

These acts prohibited interstate commerce in any food, drug, or cosmetic that was adulterated or misbranded. The FDA was charged with ensuring that foods, drugs, and cosmetics are not poisonous or harmful to health, are not decayed, filthy, or putrid, and do not contain a harmful chemical or dangerous substance. The agency is also responsible for ensuring that labels warn consumers of the health dangers of a product, do not claim curative powers the product does not have, are truthful, and do not represent the product as being something other than what it is. In order to fulfill its mission, the agency performs a variety of tasks, including the inspection of food processing plants, the approval of new drugs and medical devices for marketing, and the monitoring of cosmetics.

The 1938 act was especially important because it gave the FDA authority to determine that new drugs are safe before they can be marketed. This power requires the agency to approve a product before it can be marketed. Without the premarket approval requirement, products can be sold to consumers, and the FDA has to find that the product is unsafe before it can get a court order to pull the product from the market. In the 1950s premarket approval was extended to chemicals that leave residues on fruits and vegetables, chemical additives in foods, and color additives in foods, drugs, and cosmetics. The FDA determines that these substances are safe for use, and it establishes standards governing their use in particular products.

Since 1938 important changes have been made in the FDA's authority. In 1958 Congress adopted the Delaney clause, an amendment to the Food, Drug, and Cosmetic Act that bans any food additive known to cause cancer in human beings or animals. While the Delaney clause appears straightforward, its implementation is complex and conflictual. Determining that an additive causes cancer is a difficult task, and the research efforts of government and academicians are frequently criticized. In addition, food producers as well as consumers are easily upset when a favorite product is removed from the market. Conflicts over the Delaney clause plagued the FDA in the 1970s and 1980s.

Another important addition to the FDA's powers occurred in 1962 when the Food, Drug, and Cosmetic Act was amended to require the FDA to determine that the drugs are effective as well as safe. Thus, to be marketed a drug has to do what the manufacturer claims it does; a drug that is safe but not effective cannot be marketed. This is a tremendous task for the FDA. Complaints about the drug approval process come from all sides, including those who say the agency is too slow, too fast, excessively cautious, or flagrantly careless.

The Food and Drug Administration can easily be classified as an agency administering protective regulatory policy.[2] Such a classification, however, does little to help us understand the nature of the relationships between the agency and its congressional committees. According to the typology of subgovernment analysis, protective regulatory issues are more conflictual than distributive policies, and the conflict occurs because the issues are more likely to be addressed on the floor of Congress in a partisan setting.[3] Even if this were an accurate description of regulatory policy, it does not inform us about the relationship between agencies and committees.

Another approach to regulatory policy, agency capture theory, centers on the question of what group a regulatory agency really serves, rather than what interest it is authorized to serve. This theory argues that agencies eventually make policy decisions that benefit the businesses they are expected to regulate because they operate in an environment providing little support for a strict regulatory approach.[4] The explanation for this outcome focuses on interest groups. Groups representing businesses are organized and politically active; groups representing the public are not. The legislature's response to the agency's actions tends to be ignored. The presumption is usually that the legislature does not know or does not care that the agency is captured by the business it is supposed to regulate. Thus, the work on agency capture affords few insights about the rise and fall of conflict and consensus between an agency and its authorizing committees.

The relationships between the FDA and its authorizing committees conform to the policy model rather than the self-interest model or the subgovernment variant. Frequent conflicts developed as both the committees and the FDA tried to promote their own views of desirable and necessary policy. The committees maintained a strong and active interest in the enabling legislation of the agency as well as the way in which the FDA implemented that legislation. Frequent congressional oversight tried to push the agency to be more, not less, protective of consumers. The agency was often attacked for poor management and judgment that resulted in a failure to safeguard consumers from harmful foods and drugs. Despite this oversight, the agency did not always support the legislation pushed by the committees. Nor did the committees always endorse the regulatory measures developed by the agency. Disputes emerged as the agency fought for greater discretion and the committees tried to exert more control over agency actions.

Consistent with the hypotheses of the policy model, the center of these disputes was the committee, not the floor of Congress. Table 4.1 shows few roll-call votes on FDA programs during the twenty-four years studied. The frequent conflicts between the committees and the agencies rarely spilled over to the House and Senate chambers. Conflict was rarely generated by outsiders, but issues were raised easily by committee members and FDA officials. Each dispute was confined to the issue at hand—the system was loosely coupled—so conflicts did not fracture the subgovernment and tumble to the floor.

The FDA interacts with several congressional committees, and three primary authorizing committees were selected for this analysis. They were the House Commerce Committee, the Senate Labor and Public

Table 4.1

Number of Roll-Call Votes on Programs Administered by the Food and Drug Administration in the House and Senate, 1961 to 1984

Year	House	Senate
1961	0	0
1962	0	1
1963	0	0
1964	0	0
1965	0	0
1966	0	5
1967	2	0
1968	1	0
1969	0	0
1970	0	0
1971	1	2
1972	3	4
1973	0	0
1974	0	0
1975	0	4
1976	1	0
1977	0	0
1978	0	0
1979	0	0
1980	0	0
1981	0	0
1982	0	0
1983	0	0
1984	5	0

Source: Roll-call votes were collected from the *Congressional Quarterly Almanac*, volumes dated from 1961 to 1984. Votes needed a ten-percent dissent rate, the standard rate for roll-call analysis, to be counted.

Welfare Committee,[5] and the House Government Operations Committee. The House Government Operations Committee was included because of the dominant role the Intergovernmental Relations Subcommittee played in investigating the agency's management practices. At times other committees are mentioned because of their involvement in a specific issue.

The Regulation of Drugs

Throughout the 1960s, congressional committees criticized the FDA's administrative procedures, especially in the area of drug regulation. At the same time, however, the agency and the committees agreed on legislation providing additional authority to the agency. The members wanted the FDA to be more aggressive and move more quickly and certainly; the criticisms were attempts to push the agency in that direction. The agency, forced to shift from an inspection-oriented to a scientific, research-oriented bureau, responded, albeit somewhat slowly, to these directives. A consensus on legislation emerged because the agency accepted the additional responsibilities as solutions to problems uncovered by investigations of agency practices. Yet the committees' desire to push for stronger regulatory efforts was not unlimited. When the agency proposed more strenuous and comprehensive regulations on certain kinds of drugs at the end of the decade, legislators complained vociferously about them. The committees wanted aggressive regulation but not too much of it, and the agency had to uncover where that line was supposed to be drawn.

The FDA agreed to the legislative proposals offered by the congressional committees in the 1960s. The most significant legislation requiring the most substantial programmatic change for the FDA was the Kefauver–Harris amendments, adopted in 1962. These amendments significantly changed the criteria used to determine whether drugs could be marketed. Earlier law required only that drugs be safe; the Kefauver–Harris amendments stipulated that drugs be effective as well as safe in order to be marketed. On the surface, this change seemed simple. But the new criterion demanded a significantly different determination about a drug.[6] Before deciding that a drug could be marketed, the FDA had to determine whether or not it accomplished its goal—whether it was efficacious—not merely whether or not it was safe.

Passed unanimously by Congress, the extensive support for the bill was created largely by Senator Estes Kefauver's (D–TN) use of the thalidomide crisis. A drug found to cause birth defects, thalidomide had not been approved for marketing in the United States. But it had almost been approved for marketing; one FDA official intervened to veto the request. The uncovering of both the drug's side effects and the FDA's drug approval process was used by Kefauver to generate support for further strengthening the FDA's regulation of drugs. A weaker bill would have passed without the discovery of the thalidomide problem, but the incident created a situation in which it was difficult for legislators to oppose toughening the drug laws.

The FDA supported the Kefauver–Harris amendments, but its support was not enthusiastic. The agency accepted the changes, but it did not promote them. The amendments were advanced primarily by Kefauver's urging and tenacity. Kefauver used his position as chair of the Antitrust and Monopoly Subcommittee of the Senate Judiciary Committee to advance a policy solution of substantial interest to him. The FDA as well as the Kennedy Administration followed but did not lead Kefauver. They were probably willing to settle for the less stringent regulations that would have emerged in the absence of the thalidomide crisis.

Considering the changes the agency had to make to adapt to the new demands placed on it by the Kefauver–Harris amendments, it is somewhat surprising that the FDA did not react more negatively to the proposal. Legislative oversight helped set up the idea that problems existed, and Kefauver stepped in with the solution to those problems. The notion that the FDA had serious problems, both with the law as written and with the way it was implemented, was effectively developed at a series of congressional hearings. The Kefauver subcommittee began investigating the drug industry in 1959. In 1960 concerned employees testified about the agency's practices at the hearings, and the discovery of improprieties of one employee raised questions about the agency's ties with industry.

Congressional attention to agency decisions did not wane after the bill was adopted. The committees continued to watch the FDA, checking its implementation of the Kefauver–Harris amendments. Kefauver died in 1963, but Representative L.H. Fountain (D–NC) quickly picked up the oversight function. His House Government Operations Subcommittee on Intergovernmental Relations uncovered many instances in which the approval of new drugs and the regulation of drugs after they were marketed were handled carelessly and incompletely. The Fountain subcommittee dogged the FDA in a series of hearings in 1964, 1965, and 1966, highlighting the inadequate implementation of the Kefauver–Harris amendments and laxness in relying on up-to-date scientific information.

Although appropriations quadrupled between 1956 and 1964 and positions for enforcement operations more than tripled,[7] the agency initially had little programmatic response to the numerous criticisms that continued after the 1962 law.[8] Top personnel, as they did in the 1950s, placed their faith in the industry and relied primarily on voluntary compliance. In the past, the agency had emphasized inspection of food and drug manufacturers as a major way to protect consumers.

With the adoption of the Kefauver–Harris amendments, the FDA had to shift its emphasis to scientific research. The congressional interest helped promote this change because it established an environment favoring more aggressive action by the agency. According to FDA Commissioner George Larrick, the agency could correct controls over the distribution and use of investigational drugs through regulatory measures after the thalidomide scandal and the 1962 amendments because it then had the right public attitude, public attention, and congressional interest to allow stricter action.[9]

Stronger support for a legislative program developed in the mid-1960s when the FDA acquired new leadership, President Johnson targeted consumer protection as a priority in domestic policy, and congressional committees continued to promote stricter regulation. In 1966 the new commissioner, James Goddard, adopted a more adversarial posture toward business, beginning his term with several speeches attacking the drug industry and the pharmaceutical associations.[10] At the same time, President Johnson found that consumer protection legislation could meet both his desire for new social programs and the legislature's wish to adopt no costly new programs.[11] A series of legislative initiatives was introduced in 1965 that satisfied Johnson as well as the demands that the FDA become a more aggressive protector of the American public. In 1965 Congress passed a bill to extend federal controls over psychotoxic drugs such as barbiturates and amphetamines. A truth-in-packaging bill and a Child Protection Act were both passed without controversy in 1966. The House Commerce Committee acted on additional measures to streamline premarketing clearance of animal drugs and upgrade the FDA's training programs. Because the agency was not unwilling to take on or advocate new responsibilities, consensus developed with the committees pushing for more aggressive leadership.

The complaints about poor management waned somewhat when the legislative initiatives were perceived as a way to redress the problems. Yet all of this activity only temporarily decreased congressional criticism of the agency. Concern about the agency's management emerged again in 1969. This time it was the agency's own study that caused the commotion. An internal report concluded that the agency did not adequately protect the consumer because of insufficient manpower, legislative authority, and resources. The congressional response was predictable. The agency's program, mission, and priorities were investigated in congressional hearings, with ensuing declarations that at the very least new authority would be forthcoming.[12] Administration responses were more immediate. Most of the top personnel, including the commissioner, were replaced, and the agency was once again reorganized, this time into product-related bureaus.[13]

These conflicts developed because the committees pushed a somewhat reluctant agency to alter its orientation. The FDA's willingness to accept new tasks seemed to be a response to the congressional criticisms. Often these new responsibilities were suggested by the legislature, not the agency. There is little evidence that the agency acted like an entrepreneur; there was little programmatic response to the congressional criticisms until after Commissioner Goddard was selected in 1966. The FDA was oriented toward inspection, not research activities, and the committees were trying to change agency behavior. Consistent with the notion of "problemistic search,"[14] the frequent hearings stimulated some search for and acceptance of new alternatives because they indicated to the agency that serious problems existed. The agency had difficulties adapting to these changes, as evidenced by the problems cited in the congressional hearings.

An alternative view of these events is that the agency had little incentive to correct the legislative perception that it made mistakes. Legislators who want an agency to take stronger regulatory actions would not want to cut the agency's resources; to the contrary, they would respond to complaints of incompetence by increasing the resources available to the bureau.[15] An agency intent on maximizing its budget would see the criticisms as a potential gold mine because they could be used to generate more revenue. A destructive cycle could emerge, in which legislators provided more funds but administrators continued their lackadaisical regulatory actions.

This is a somewhat perverse strategy and also an extremely risky tactic for an agency. The danger is that agency supporters could become disgusted, convinced that the bureau would never be improved. Legislators would turn their attention and support away from the bureau. The FDA encountered precisely this response. In the early 1970s the Senate Labor and Public Welfare and the Senate Commerce committees endorsed a bill that would have established a Consumer Safety Agency and transferred FDA functions to the new bureau. The Consumer Safety Agency was never created, but sections of the FDA were transferred to another new agency, the Consumer Product Safety Commission. The dominant concern was that the FDA was not adequately administering existing laws and certainly could not be given any new responsibilities to protect consumers. Even the House Commerce Committee, a committee that was not very active in consumer issues, was reluctant "to assign substantial additional responsibilities to FDA in the face of a series of studies in recent years which have been sharply critical of the agency's ability to carry out effectively the responsibilities already assigned to it."[16] Although the House Commerce Committee did not want to give the FDA new tasks, it was less willing to transfer all responsibilities to the new agency. The final result was that only a few functions were moved.[17]

Even though congressional committees were calling for more aggressive regulation, the FDA encountered considerable resistance when it tried to regulate combination drugs. The FDA's concern was that combination drugs, two or more drugs joined into one dosage, were not necessarily more effective. Because drugs have side effects and individuals develop immunities to some of them, the FDA did not want consumers to take drugs that were not necessary. The agency's move to regulate the drugs was consistent with the push from Congress to implement the Kefauver–Harris amendments.

Yet in 1971 the FDA was forced to ease the regulations covering combination prescription and nonprescription drugs that it had been preparing over the previous few years. Hearings by the House Commerce and Government Operations committees as well as a letter to the Secretary of HEW signed by 100 members and accompanied by phone calls from fifty more legislators prompted the agency to back down and submit less stringent regulations.[18] Legislators responded to the concerns of the drug industry that claimed that the guidelines were a threat to ban all combination drugs, a large percentage of prescription and most over-the-counter drugs. Only one professional organization, which was not active in the legislative debate, supported the guidelines. Similarly, only a few legislators publicly expressed approval of the rules.[19]

In agency–committee relationships throughout the 1960s, the dispute over combination drugs is the one conflict that was initiated by the bureaucracy; an agency pressing for stricter regulation encountered the opposition of legislators reluctant to support such changes. The interesting point about this particular situation, though, is that the legislative pressures throughout the decade were to tighten and strengthen regulations, and the central problem was the agency's failure to press for additional authority. But when the FDA took a major step to do that, its plans faced considerable criticism. Because the agency did not have the resources to counter the opposition, or at least the willingness to expend them, it had to make concessions. Of course, one could argue that the congressional complaints were symbolic, that legislators found it useful to complain about lax regulation but had no real desire to endure the costs of stricter action. Because the committees had pushed actively for new legislation, this assessment seems a bit weak. It is more likely that the members tried to balance competing interests because they had to respond to the demands of groups on both sides of the question of how much regulation there should be. Rather than hold a particular stance in the face of opposition, the committees adjusted policy, depending on which side yelled the loudest. If the agency wanted to minimize conflict by responding to congressional demands, the problem it faced was deciding how the legislature would react to its proposals.

The pattern of conflict and consensus between the FDA and its authorizing committees during the 1960s initially seems confusing. There was consensus on general enabling legislation, conflict over general administrative actions, and a dispute over the regulation of a specific product. However, the policy model clarifies these interactions. Committee members maintained an active interest in FDA decision making. Oversight of the agency was neither superficial nor sporadic. Committee hearings were a thorough and persistent examination of the internal procedures used to make decisions. The knowledge gleaned from these investigations was used first to rewrite the authorizing legislation and then to push the agency to implement it. Several legislators were the key actors here, as they used their positions as subcommittee chairmen to advance specific policy issues that they decided were important. Conflict was not raised by outsiders but by the legislators as they decided to focus their time and energy on drug regulation.

Legislative initiatives such as these do not automatically generate conflict. The disputes of the 1960s emerged because the FDA adapted more slowly to the new demands of the Kefauver–Harris amendments. The committees could embrace the stricter regulatory approach quite easily. But it was the agency that had to change its internal procedures and its approach to drug regulation, and this shift from inspection to scientific research was not easy for the agency. The legislative investigations helped to stimulate this change as they pointed out problems with past decision making and prodded the agency to implement the Kefauver–Harris amendments. Unfortunately for the agency, however, the guidelines from the committees were not completely consistent, and they reigned-in the FDA when it initiated strong regulations of combination drugs.

Conflicts over New Responsibilities

In the early 1970s, after the complaints about the FDA's management waned, the Senate Labor and Public Welfare Committee and the agency clashed again but this time could not agree on a coherent legislative program. The legislators and the bureaucrats developed different views of what actions were necessary to protect the public. Both the House and the Senate committees had members who wanted a more aggressive and protectionist role for the FDA. The agency, on the other hand, balked at the intrusion and resisted the increased responsibilities and authority, as it tried to maintain its discretion and protect the integrity of its laws.

FDA Resistance to Expansion

Many members on the committees, particularly the Democrats, pushed consumer interests, a movement that had started picking up momentum in the late 1960s. Senators on the Labor and Public Welfare Committee pursued legislation that would revamp the FDA's responsibilities in foods and cosmetics. Senator Thomas Eagleton (D–MO) advocated premarket testing of cosmetics, complaining that the 1938 Food, Drug, and Cosmetic Act was "woefully inadequate" in this area and that he thought the "FDA was moving in the area of cosmetics with great lethargy, great reluctance, almost kicking and screaming."[20] Bills to monitor food processors grew out of proposals introduced in the late 1960s requiring inspection of fish and fish products. By expanding registration and surveillance requirements, the bills were the broadest revision of the laws in both of these areas since the 1938 act.

Most of these bills received support in the Senate committee and on the floor, were opposed in whole or in part by the FDA, and died in the House when there was no committee action. The agency praised the intentions of the provisions but argued that many of them were unnecessary, were too time-consuming, and would require too many re-sources. An administration bill that provided for some new authority but never went as far as the congressional bill usually was introduced as an alternative to show the agency's willingness to recognize prob-lems with current practices.

The agency completely opposed the cosmetics bills, arguing that the provisions were unnecessary as well as overly burdensome. Commis-sioner Alexander Schmidt admitted that cosmetics were a low priority in the agency but anyway asserted that the requirements of the pro-posal would overwhelm the agency:

> I have this recurring nightmare in which our building here across from HEW, which is a fairly large building, is totally inundated by small vials of cosmetics. We know of more than 10,000 products on the market, and the idea of receiving data on 10,000 products is almost enough to make one wish not to be the Commissioner of Food and Drugs, as admirable a position as that is.[21]

The proposals relating to foods were received with somewhat more warmth. Still the agency did not want to extend the stringent require-ments usually advocated in the Senate bills. The agency opposed full-time continuous inspection of fish and fish products while ac-knowledging the need for some kind of regular inspection.[22] When Senators expanded these proposals a few years later to cover food processors, the FDA had similar reservations. The commissioner testi-fied against yearly inspection of food plants as well as yearly registra-tion requirements,[23] and the agency viewed the surveillance requirements in an earlier proposal as overly burdensome procedural hurdles. The agency only gave its support to a one-time mandatory registration and stronger authority to collect information from food processing plants.

One could claim that these incidents were not conflicts between the agency and the committee at all but were disputes between the Repub-lican Nixon Administration and the Democratic legislature. The agency supported additional authority in the 1960s when under a Dem-ocratic administration, then changed its perspective with the leadership of a Republican president who favored the provision of fewer government services. The problem with this conclusion is that it is not consistent with many other events during this period. The Nixon Administration in response to criticisms of the agency supported a fifty-percent increase in the agency's budget for fiscal year 1973. It submitted measures expanding the FDA's regulatory authority over medical devices and the listing of drugs on the market, and it also proposed a "bill of rights" for consumers.

Because the House Commerce Committee never reported these bills, the question here is the extent of conflict between the FDA and the Senate Labor and Public Welfare Committee. The agency clashed with senators who were acting as entrepreneurs, seeking out new programs that meshed with the interests of an active consumer movement. The FDA did not have such an imperialist perspective. The conflict developed because the FDA did not want to adopt new responsibilities. The agency accepted a more restrained role because of its views of effective policy; current policy in foods and cosmetics was sufficient to protect consumers.

The agency's reluctance to take on these additional tasks is understandable in the context of the policy model. First, the FDA was very concerned about the integrity of its policies. The agency did not want to be given authority for tasks that it could not adequately perform. When reacting to the proposals, administrative burdens were constantly stressed. Dramatically changing the inspection requirements for food processors and the testing and clearance procedures for cosmetics would introduce considerable uncertainty in the administrative process. Criteria for the safety of cosmetics, review procedures, and inspection and surveillance procedures for foods would have to be developed. In addition, new standard operating procedures would have to be designed, upsetting existing practices. The Medical Devices Act of 1976, one supported by the agency as well as the committees at about the same time, presented the same kind of problems with uncertainty. However, a separate division was added to deal with medical devices so that new tasks did not have to fit with existing ones. With food and cosmetics, the additional responsibilities had to be worked into the current tasks and practices.

One could argue that the FDA opposed these provisions because it did not have enough resources to implement them, and indeed, that concern is apparent in testimony at hearings. Commissioner Schmidt asserted, "The thing I have to worry about most is being given additional responsibilities without the resources to carry them out."[24] But this concern would not come from a budget-maximizing agency. An agency concerned with maximizing its budget would argue that it was willing to accept the new responsibilities and then use the new tasks to justify more appropriations. The agency's objections were not presented in this manner.

Second, the FDA and the legislators had different views of the extent and severity of the problem. Although the agency expressed some sympathy with the goals that the legislators were trying to achieve,[25] it did not perceive the problems to be so serious as to warrant the legislation. This is especially the case with cosmetics. Commissioner Schmidt's responses stressed that because cosmetics were not essential for the health and well-being of the public, it would be difficult to justify the marketing of cosmetics that had any harmful side effects at all.[26] Therefore, it was important only that the public be able to make an informed choice. This attitude led to support for premarket testing but not premarket clearance of these products. In reference to the food bills, an FDA official expressed his doubts about whether or not the requirements in the bill were necessary:

> The agency in terms of the science says we don't need to do all of that, it's not necessary or it can't be done. The [committee] staffers think it's the greatest thing since sliced bread, but that's because they have never had to run an agency. . . . We say, hey, we've got enough to do right now without doing any more. We have to keep our scientists up to date. And we can't do that well because we're too busy doing inspections. A case in point is fish inspections. Do we really need to do that?[27]

Conflict arose, then, as the committees and the agency differed over the need for legislation.

Convincing an agency that a serious problem needs attention seems to be an important precursor to its endorsement of a change in policy. The FDA did not always oppose change. Changes were sought and accepted when search was spurred by problems raised by congressional committees.[28] The Drug Division accepted a number of new responsibilities in the 1960s, especially with the adoption of the Kefauver–Harris amendments in 1962. It seems likely that the considerable number of hearings held on drug regulation as well as specific examples of harm caused by particular drugs triggered both the recognition that a problem needed to be mitigated and searches for new alternatives. In the area of medical devices the agency was stimulated to address the problem by the growing use and numbers of devices as well as a law that left the question of their regulation rather vague. In addition to this, a problem with intrauterine devices was uncovered, and Representative Fountain's subcommittee as well as the Senate Labor and Public Welfare Committee held hearings on the birth control devices.

With the food and cosmetics bills, however, relatively few hearings were held, and not many incidents suggested there was a particular problem. The only hearings held on cosmetics were those addressing the specific bills; there were no hearings on particular problems with current practices. Aside from food additives, which is a separate issue, there were only two hearings on the regulation of the food industry. The House Commerce Committee held a brief hearing on recall procedures after a botulism outbreak from Bon Vivant soups,[29] and a more complete investigation of the Food Division of the agency in 1972.[30] The agency had no particular reason to believe there was a serious problem that needed consideration, and it was not induced to search for or contemplate changes in existing practices. Finally, the agency opposed the bills because of the detailed and strict procedures that were outlined by Congress. In the early 1970s the legislature wrote several specific requirements for regulatory agencies into statutes in an attempt to reduce administrative discretion and tighten the regulation of industry.[31] The bills in these instances fit with that practice. But the FDA developed its own perspectives of what was and was not necessary and did not want procedures to be stipulated by Congress. An FDA official outlined some of these concerns:

> Here again, Congress was being too specific about what they wanted us to do. There was a whole list of very specific things, finite things written in the statute. That started out as the Dangerous Materials bill with Magnuson and Hart, then it kind of got side-tracked. They wanted lists of everything, complete surveillance, and intensive screening. . . . Our concern is that we can't protect everybody from everything, and we don't want to be excessive.[32]

The FDA bases many of its decisions on scientific findings and many of its employees are professional scientists. Thus, it is not surprising that it wanted discretion to provide greater freedom to its professional staff and opposed attempts by legislators to tighten up on the rules and regulations.

The Regulation of Medical Devices

Because Medical Devices was established as a separate division of the FDA, meshing new practices with old was not a significant problem and there was not as much concern with uncertainty. The FDA supported the medical devices amendment, so there was consensus with the committees when the amendment was initially adopted in 1976. Despite the fact that the law contained very detailed provisions that limited the agency's discretion, the FDA initially supported the law. As the agency began to implement it, however, enthusiasm waned. Administrators recognized that the provisions hampered their exercise of discretion. The law included very specific procedures for the regulation of different classes of medical devices. Because of the rapid increase in the number of devices as well as the stringent requirements of the law, the agency had considerable difficulty implementing the provisions. Six years after the adoption of the amendments, the agency wanted to increase its discretion by simplifying the law, and it clashed with congressional committees that criticized the agency's failure to implement the congressional guidelines.

In 1982 and 1983 the House Commerce Committee investigated the FDA's failure to make much headway in administering the 1976 medical devices amendments.[33] An agency official reenacted the difficulty the agency had at the hearings:

> And you know how many standards we have? We have none. What do you say at a hearing? You go into the hearings, and the congressman says, "*How* many standards do you have developed?" And you fumble around and say, "let me look at my notes, well, we have zero." And they say, "*Zero?* Out of 1,100? The law was passed in 1976." So you say, "Well, we have ten that are about ready." And they say, "ten? out of 1,100?"[34]

Calling medical devices the FDA's neglected child, the subsequent report chastised the agency for not completing in six years what Congress wanted finished in one year. It blamed the lack of implementation rather than the statutory scheme for the delays.[35]

As the agency developed more expertise about medical devices, a sense that it could decide what action was necessary at what times emerged. The bureau developed an independent assessment of the necessary action, and the congressional provisions became burdensome constraints rather than useful guidelines:

> In 1976 the performance standards made sense. But it is naive to think that everything had to have standards. . . . It takes three to four years to do a standard. We figured it would take 100 percent of our staff for twenty years just to do the one thing. . . . The special tests for colors have to be submitted to the old Bureau of Foods, even though we have this process over here. And it takes forever. The law says we have to do this. Why should colors be tested separately? Are they any more harmful than anything else? Probably not. The system is kind of dumb. We ignore it for the most part. That means we're in conflict with the law, and Congress will say we're not administering the law.[36]

Because the legislators were not concerned about increasing discretion and saw nothing wrong with the statutory scheme, the agency clashed with the committee. The hearings elicited some positive responses from the FDA. The division that handled medical devices was strengthened, and the issue was given more priority within the agency. Agency officials were still wishing, though, that legislative changes would be made to ease the stiff requirements of the law. Administrators had slim hopes that Congress would take the time to change the law; as one official said, "comforting the bureaucracy isn't very important on the Hill."[37]

Regulating Vitamins and Minerals

Although the Senate Labor and Public Welfare Committee wanted the agency to move more aggressively in this area, again there was a limit to what the committee would endorse. Like the dispute in the early 1970s over combination drugs, the FDA went too far in the eyes of the committee when it tried to regulate the sale of vitamins and minerals. The FDA saw these products as a waste of consumer's money at best and harmful to individuals at worst.

The dispute developed in 1973 when the FDA issued regulations to protect consumers from the harmful effects of taking large doses of vitamins and minerals. After various health food and pharmaceutical groups promptly protested, the Senate committee responded to those complaints. Senators William Proxmire (D–WI) and Robert Schweiker (R–PA), who introduced proposals limiting FDA action, argued that the dosage guidelines were arbitrary and unscientific. In 1974 and again in 1975, the Senate committee barred the FDA from regulating the composition or maximum potency of vitamins and minerals except in certain circumstances.[38] The Senate measure limited FDA regulations and placed the burden of proving the danger of the substances on the agency. Although committee members had been stressing additional protection for the American consumer, they balked at FDA efforts to regulate vitamins and minerals. The members listened to those who had to pay the costs of the regulation. This time, though, it was a burden that the American public did not want to bear.

The self-interest model predicts that consensus between the agencies and the committees would have emerged during this time. A budget-maximizing agency would support the proposals for new tasks in hopes of using the additional responsibilities to generate greater appropriations. If anything, the agency would have tried to stimulate greater interest and action by the House Commerce Committee, a body that showed little interest in passing these proposals. But the FDA resisted the new tasks, producing conflict rather than consensus with the Senate Labor and Public Welfare Committee.

Although these disputes make little sense in the context of the self-interest model, they are accounted for by the policy model. Because the FDA and the committee developed different views of the severity of the problem, they did not agree on the need for solutions. The agency had its own priorities and did not see any reason to get excited about the proposals. In fact, the agency had every reason to oppose them because the requirements seemed overly burdensome and unmanageable. The FDA wanted to protect the integrity of its policies, not open itself up to criticisms when it could not implement an unwieldy law. Finally, although these disputes center around the scope of authority held by the agency, they also involve the exercise of that authority. If granted new tasks, the FDA wanted greater discretion to set up its standard operating procedures. But the committees, echoing the view that regulatory agencies had too much freedom, sought to exert greater control over agency decision-making processes.

Food Additives and the Delaney Clause

A persistent controversy over food additives arose in the early 1970s. Although the intensity of this debate has varied since then, the underlying dilemma has never been resolved. The FDA was prevented from acting on one substance, hounded about its inaction on another, and generally batted about by those on both sides of the issue as members of Congress waffled. For their part, agency officials said they wanted a law that was reasonable, workable, and defensible according to both available science and current public opinion. In the words of one official, "we don't want to appear dumb." Unfortunately for the agency, the legislature did not reach a consensus about whether the law should be changed or how it should be altered.

The legislation creating this uproar is commonly called the Delaney clause, named after Congressman James Delaney (D–NY), who initiated it. Adopted in 1958, the clause states that any food additive which is shown to cause cancer in human beings or animals must be banned without considering the benefits that might occur from the use of the additive. Because of technological testing improvements, smaller and smaller particles of an additive can now be detected in a food. The problem these tests create is that the disparity between the amount consumed in the average diet and the amount used in research tests can be so large as to appear ridiculous. The FDA encountered precisely such a situation when it announced in connection with the impending ban of saccharin that the amount given to the rats in the tests was equivalent to a person drinking 800 twelve-ounce cans of diet soda per day. Scientific analysis is beginning to show the risks associated with the various amounts of an additive, but it cannot determine whether that risk is worth taking.

The banning of cyclamates, an artificial sweetener, in 1969 by the agency was the initial step in this persistent issue. Although there were motions to compensate producers of cyclamates,[39] there was no movement to repeal the ban and relatively little discussion about the rigidity and unreasonableness of the Delaney clause. Instead what little movement occurred was in the direction of strengthening the regulations. The identification of cyclamates as a carcinogen raised doubts about other commonly used food additives. President Nixon requested a thorough review of the substances on a list called GRAS, "generally regarded as safe," because cyclamates had been on that list. The Senate Committee on Nutrition and Human Needs, headed by Gaylord Nelson (D–WI), held hearings on a bill that would have broadened the definition of a food additive and extended the Delaney clause to cover additional negative effects of additives.

The conflict at the time was over FDA inaction; the Senate Labor and Public Welfare Committee chastised the FDA for moving too slowly in removing diethylstilbestrol (DES) from the food supply of cattle. A hormone that increased growth in cattle, DES had sometimes been given to pregnant women and was associated with cancer in their children. The Senate committee passed a bill providing for an immediate ban on DES in 1972 and again in 1975; there was no House action. Although the FDA had tried to ban DES in 1972, a court ruling overturned the ban, and the agency did not try to reinstate it. The committee acted because it did not think the ban proposed by the FDA was strong enough. The ban stopped production yet permitted the use of existing supplies of DES.[40] Initially, then, dissatisfaction with the FDA stemmed from beliefs that it moved too slowly, not too fast, in removing potentially carcinogenic additives from the market.

The tide turned a few years later when the FDA proposed a ban on saccharin, the only low-calorie sweetener available. Described by one official as "the largest mail-writing campaign since the Vietnam War,"[41] Congress and the agency were swamped with letters from individuals opposing the ban and outlining their need for the sweetener. With little hesitation, Congress prevented the FDA from enforcing the Delaney clause and prohibited a ban on the sale of saccharin, extending its use for another two years. A jurisdictional squabble erupted between the authorizations and appropriations committees about who should impose the ban. Senator Edward Kennedy (D–MA) made some feeble attempts to delay congressional action, and a warning label was required on products using the additive. However, there was very little opposition to the prohibition of the ban. After that initial action in 1977, almost every two years Congress routinely extended the prohibition on the ban of saccharin.

One could argue that this apparent conflict was merely symbolic, that actually no conflict between the committees and the agency developed over saccharin because the agency did not really want to remove the additive from the market. The way in which the agency announced its action against saccharin led some to question its sincerity and argue that the agency acted only because the Delaney clause required it to.[42] Some officials in the agency felt the data supported a ban on saccharin based on other food laws, and others did not. There was, however, consensus that the Delaney clause itself mandated a ban. FDA administrators acknowledged that the agency did not handle the proposal very well and generally described it as a public relations gaffe:

> They did some dumb things with that. I can say that because I wasn't
> here then. That 800 bottles bit. That was some public relations person
> trying to explain how things were done. It was irrelevant to the whole
> issue. Then we were Carsonized [*Q*. What?] Johnny Carson started
> telling jokes about us. Once that happens, then you're dead. It was no
> longer a viable public issue.[43]

Officials were not entirely pleased with congressional action that questioned the legitimacy of the Delaney clause yet did not replace it with any other policy. The agency was stuck with a law that people felt was unreasonable but was still supposed to be enforced.

A similar situation almost arose a year later over sodium nitrites, a preservative used in meats. In cooperation with the Department of Agriculture, the agency moved somewhat more cautiously with this substance, suggesting a gradual ban on its use. At least from the agency's perspective, a ban on nitrites presented a more serious public health problem than that on saccharin because the possibility of botulism from spoiled meat seemed more harmful than an increase in caloric intake. According to the law, though, the agency did not have the option of weighing the benefits of an additive, so the use of the product had to be discontinued. As it turned out, the data in the study linking nitrites to cancer were faulty, and the ban was dropped by the agency.

These events sparked considerable debate, yet little action, about changing the food safety laws. Initially, the agency's attitude seemed to be that it had to do what the law required, and if Congress did not like it, Congress should change the law:

> The next thing that came up was nitrites. . . . Fortunately, it was not
> found to be a carcinogen. If that had happened, it would have been "all
> right, Congress. You don't like saccharin, now deal with nitrites."[44]

As time passed, and there was no congressional action, the agency moved closer to administrative solutions, even though officials believed that altering the law should be a legislative responsibility. Some court cases gave the agency more discretion in implementing the Delaney clause. Yet agency officials felt that Congress should be the institution to change the law because it was the legislature's responsibility to set broad policy guidelines for the agency as well as to determine what risks were socially acceptable. They complained about the situation, arguing that Congress abandoned its responsibility to set a policy direction for the agency:

> One person is saying why are you wasting the money, someone else at the same time is saying why aren't you doing more? They'll write a bill that is supposed to be unequivocal but gives us leeway. Some of them were telling us that the Delaney clause is absolute, but you have discretion in the color additives issue. What is a socially acceptable risk? That is not up to the agency to decide, let Congress do it. But they don't want to do it because they don't want the responsibility. They'll let the agency do it and then they'll complain. . . . It doesn't give us any direction about where we're supposed to go. The agency just drifts. We don't know where to go. They'll tell us to rewrite a bill and when we get it right, they'll know.[45]

Although the agency did not take an official position on altering the Delaney clause, there was a consensus that it should be changed. Bureau officials viewed the clause as unworkable and felt that it no longer provided adequate guidelines for decisions. The fact that the Delaney clause formally allows no discretion did not protect the agency from criticism. Any decision the agency made about a substance was accompanied by controversy, different interpretations of the data, and accusations that the agency was not protecting the public's health and safety or that it was protecting it too much. Decisions justified only by the Delaney clause and not by other food laws were questioned by those outside the agency. Most administrators felt that a different law would provide more credibility and enable the agency to defend its decisions better:

> We're going to have criticism no matter what, whether they change the Delaney clause or not. Changing the food safety law would provide some credibility to the law. Many decisions are seen as the FDA doing this because the Delaney clause says we have to. If we take out that rigidity, we could say we made a decision on these particular sets of data and these particular conclusions.[46]

Bills to amend the food safety laws were introduced in Congress almost every year along with various predictions about the possibility of action. Many factors inhibited legislative overhaul of the Delaney clause, especially when a case-by-case approach was possible. First, no obvious technical solution emerged. There was a fair amount of consensus that the Delaney clause needed to be changed; there was little consensus about what it should be changed to. Making policy about the socially acceptable level of risk is full of uncertainty and not full of information. Combined with that is the fact that a decision to alter the Delaney clause to allow carcinogenic substances could have severe consequences. If a carcinogenic substance were allowed on the market and later caused serious health problems, Congress would probably be attacked for not protecting the public's health.

Second, the politics of the issue provided little incentive to key legislators to act. Many consumer groups opposed any changes to the Delaney clause because they did not trust the agency, particularly during the Reagan Administration, to administer a law with more discretion. Legislators who wanted to protect consumers through strict regulatory action did not know what changes in the clause would further that policy goal. Also, ideological differences between members on these committees was high, and these same legislators felt that rewriting the food safety laws could lead to a plethora of undesirable, yet not trivial, alterations:

> We haven't moved forward on any food laws out of fear that once you're moving on a food bill, it becomes uncontrollable. [Senator] Hatch, in the last Congress on the generic drug law, showed he could be reasonable. But we don't have any confidence that he will be reasonable. There is no confidence that if we go to conference, we'll get something reasonable.[47]

Dealing with these issues on a case-by-case basis was a good policy-making approach for the legislators, especially when the alternative was to venture into a complicated, seemingly unending maze. Handling each case as it came up helped to maintain and resolve conflict. It allowed legislators to balance conflicting goals without having to face the contradictions head-on. It produced outcomes that were convenient for consumers yet probably not harmful.

The legislature was content to retain the Delaney clause in the absence of a consensus on an alternative because exempting specific substances from the clause was an acceptable compromise. For the agency, however, this case-by-case approach undermined the legitimacy of the law it was forced to implement. The agency had to invoke the Delaney clause when it was warranted, yet it knew that its decisions would be questioned, especially when the use of the additive provided some benefits. Thus, the agency was often reluctant to ban substances, as illustrated by the delay in banning DES, the presentation of the saccharin ban, and the proposed gradual ban of sodium nitrites. However, this tentative approach did not bolster the legitimacy of the agency's action because it was often interpreted as an indication that the action was unwarranted or that the FDA did not take very seriously its responsibility of protecting consumers.

One might think that the Delaney clause would protect the agency from criticism because it mandates specific action and does not allow the agency to determine what should be done in a particular case. If an agency is required by law to take a specific action, it hardly seems fair to criticize it when it does. But the Delaney clause did not prevent debates about the decisions leading up to its use, and it opened up the issue of its legitimacy whenever it was followed. Agency officials all pointed out that questions about the data, debates over conclusions, and complaints about the agency's judgment continued despite the clear and specific guideline for administrative actions. The agency had no strategy to follow to try to minimize these disputes. Because there was no consensus within Congress or even the relevant committees, any step the agency took would upset someone. The issue could not be disaggregated, so the agency did not have the opportunity to make concessions to some while appeasing others in a different way. Thus, the FDA had no way to build a supportive coalition.

Agency officials preferred to see the Delaney clause replaced by a more defensible policy with greater discretion. Because the criticisms would continue with or without the law, a more versatile provision would be more defensible and result in better policy decisions, at least from the FDA's perspective. Several administrators were very pleased with the greater flexibility provided to the FDA by judicial interpretations of the clause. But they wanted Congress to change the policy. The policy would have greater legitimacy if the legislature addressed the difficult questions of what risks should be allowed in our society.

Food additives are not the only products plagued by this problem of special exemptions. Members of Congress occasionally seek exemptions from the drug laws to allow the marketing of specific drugs. Laetrile and heroin are the two drugs which have recently received the most attention, but neither can be approved for marketing. Laetrile has not been shown to be effective in fighting cancer; heroin is illegal. The FDA resisted exemptions for both of these drugs on the grounds that they were not warranted and that they undermined the legitimacy of the drug laws.

This conflict over food additives, as well as debates over exemptions for specific drugs, fits well with the policy model. The agency's authority to regulate these products was not at issue, but the exercise of that authority was. In order to have a defensible and legitimate policy, the FDA wanted Congress to revise the Delaney clause so that the agency had more discretion. Not forced to confront the problems of implementation, legislators had no reason to jump into the murky waters of altering the provision. They were content to make decisions on a case-by-case basis, but FDA administrators saw these exemptions as questioning their judgment and undermining their authority.

Questions of Management

Like the Bureau of Indian Affairs and unlike the Bureau of Reclamation, the Food and Drug Administration underwent considerable congressional oversight throughout the 1970s and 1980s. This was particularly true in the area of drug regulation; there was less oversight of foods, and hardly any attention was paid to cosmetics. Most of these issues have already been discussed, as they often were directly linked to proposed legislative changes. Oversight sparked the agency to pay more attention to an issue, induced it to search for and consider solutions to problems, and made it more willing to support changes.

Negative effects of oversight are apparent as well. The major problem, at least from the congressional perspective, is that agency officials did not always respond to the criticisms raised in congressional oversight. The mere fact that members complained did not automatically produce changes in agency actions. Complying with legislators' wishes was not an end in itself, especially because agency officials developed their own views of what needed to be done and how it should be accomplished. The agency received feedback from a variety of different places, and congressional concerns were only one source of information. An official in one division elaborated:

> We hear the criticism from Congress, and that is most important because it is coming from the people and because they appropriate the

money and hold hearings. But we also hear about what the medical profession doesn't like, the industry criticizes us, the consumer representatives—the Sydney Wolfes [Wolfe was director of the Public Citizen Health Research Group]—criticize us. We collect these criticisms and try to come up with a balance, try to determine what is being said. Once we've listed all the criticisms, we'll see if it is legitimate. For example, the industry could be self-serving; they just want us to disappear.[48]

Although congressional reactions were important, they had to be weighed along with responses from several other interests. One significant group was the expert public, other scientists and physicians who worked in these areas:

We're responsible to the public, but we're most accountable to the expert public, and they're the more knowledgeable about what we're doing. We pay attention to the experts in these fields and what they think. We have expert advisory committees. They are nothing more than a window to the other scientists.[49]

Officials also said it was difficult to follow congressional wishes because often there was little agreement among members:

We can't be overly influenced by what one committee thinks. It's not going to do us any good. If there is unanimity, then that's one thing. But that doesn't happen very often. We do just about everything well in one quarter and poorly in another.[50]

Written and formal congressional action, such as a bill or report, received more attention because it could be used to try to determine congressional intent. The written record became the correct account when people turned back to debates for information.

There were times when agency officials decided that the legislators were wrong and that the agency should not comply with congressional requests. Bureau officials said they would try to explain why they disagreed with the legislators and what steps the agency was taking in the area under discussion. In committee hearings on a bill, for example, it was not unusual to see pages of agency testimony, not about the bill, but about the actions the agency took to deal with the problem addressed by the legislation. This was certainly the case with the legislation on foods and cosmetics in the 1970s; the obvious implication is that the legislation was not necessary because the problem was being treated administratively.

Questions about the effectiveness of congressional oversight arose when agency officials felt that legislators were not sincere in their complaints and were attacking the agency only for political reasons. Several FDA administrators were very disgruntled with congressional oversight, arguing that members were interested in publicity rather than seriously concerned about correcting a problem:

> The function of congressional hearings is to provide useful information for congressional action. But they're not useful for one whit. Ninety percent or more of the hearings are simply useless. They're a circus, a publicity event. They don't listen to the bureaucrats. They're more interested in getting publicity than in doing something useful. . . . I swear some of them practice that pointing finger in front of the mirror. I know I'm cynical, but they shouldn't use people who are just trying to do their jobs.[51]

When agency officials felt the complaints were primarily political, unrealistic, or frivolous, they were more likely to dismiss them. The dilemma, of course, is that often legislators use the oversight hearings to gain media attention and to convince the public that they are considering a critical problem, even when they sincerely *do* want to correct that problem. Foods and especially drugs lend themselves to this very nicely because the relatives of injured and deceased individuals can always appear at the hearings to dramatize the problem. However, agency officials may perceive these as primarily political proceedings and be less willing to take the members seriously.

Persistent congressional criticism did not weaken the FDA as much as it did the Bureau of Indian Affairs. The complaints about the FDA coincided with general support for food and drug regulation and came primarily from members who wanted the agency to be more protective of consumers. The criticisms of the Bureau of Indian Affairs accompanied questions about the existence of the agency and various attempts to eliminate the bureau or reduce the number of its personnel. Although there was a discussion of transferring some FDA responsibilities to a new agency, this developed because of a concern that the agency was not strong enough to protect consumers, not because the role of the bureau was in doubt.

Concluding Thoughts

During the twenty-four years covered by this study, there was an underlying agreement that regulation of food and drugs was necessary and that it was a responsibility of the federal government. Even during the move to deregulate in the late 1970s and early 1980s, the FDA was relatively immune from presidential and congressional attempts to weaken regulatory agencies. Unlike the BIA and the Bureau of Reclamation, the mission of the FDA was not seriously questioned. Yet this agreement on the need for at least some regulation did not protect the agency from disputes with congressional committees.

Conflicts between the FDA and its authorizing committees occurred fairly often throughout this period. Legislators maintained an active interest in FDA decision making. Oversight of the agency's drug division was neither superficial nor sporadic but thorough and persistent. In the 1960s consensus on new tasks for the bureau emerged as the oversight led to a search for administrative and legislative changes. But the committees' push for more aggressive regulation was limited. When the FDA tried to regulate combination drugs and vitamins and minerals, it encountered significant opposition as legislators pulled back from the aggressive, protectionist stances they had earlier taken.

The consensus on legislation broke down in the 1970s when the agency had a different perspective on appropriate policies for food and cosmetics regulation. A recognition of its administrative limitations, a desire for greater discretion, and a view that the expanded responsibilities were not necessary prompted the FDA to oppose the new tasks advocated by the Senate. The absence of hearings indicating a serious problem in food and cosmetics regulation meant that the agency was not persuaded that the policy changes were warranted.

Conflicts did not focus only on the scope of the FDA's authority but also on the way that authority was exercised. The disputes over food additives as well as exemptions for specific drugs were disputes over the discretion of the agency. The FDA sought laws whose general principles would be defensible and would not require exemptions for specific products. They wanted laws that would retain their validity in the face of controversy over particular food substances and drugs. They also wanted the legislature to be responsible for any changes made in the Delaney clause in order to uphold its legitimacy. But a case-by-case approach presented no problems for the legislators, and they did not deal with the overarching and conflictual issues of revamping the Delaney clause.

Although the FDA administers protective regulatory policy, its relationships with congressional committees were very similar to those of the Bureau of Reclamation and the Bureau of Indian Affairs. Conflict was unavoidable, but it did not fracture the subgovernment. The system was not tightly coupled; conflict on one issue did not carry over to other issues. The committees were very determined to ensure that the agency's programs were consistent with the wishes of the legislature. Although the FDA faced greater underlying support for its existence than the other agencies, it suffered from the same problem of inadequate conflict-minimizing strategies. Often there was nothing the agency could do to mitigate conflict with the committees.

Notes

1. Paul J. Quirk, "Food and Drug Administration," in James Q. Wilson, *The Politics of Regulation*, pp. 192–201.
2. Randall B. Ripley and Grace A. Franklin, *Congress, the Bureaucracy, and Public Policy*, p. 137.
3. Ibid., pp. 137–166; Theodore J. Lowi, "American Business and Public Policy, Case Studies and Political Theory"; and Robert H. Salisbury, "The Analysis of Public Policy: A Search for Theories and Roles."
4. Marver Bernstein, *Regulating Business by Independent Commission*; and Sam Peltzman, "Toward a More General Theory of Regulation," pp. 211–240.
5. This became the Senate Labor and Human Resources Committee in 1977.
6. Morton Mintz, *By Prescription Only*, p. 53.
7. William Janssen, "FDA Since 1938: The Major Trends and Developments," p. 218.
8. Mark V. Nadel, *The Politics of Consumer Protection*, pp. 68–71.
9. U.S. Congress, House Committee on Government Operations, *Hearings on Drug Safety, Part 1*, p. 177.
10. *Congressional Quarterly Almanac, 1966*, p. 347.
11. Nadel, *The Politics of Consumer Protection*, p. 40.
12. U.S. Congress, House Committee on Interstate and Foreign Commerce, Subcommittee on Public Health and Welfare, *Hearings on FDA Consumer Protection Activities—FDA Reorganization*.
13. The agency was also removed from the Consumer Protection and Environmental Health Service. *Congressional Quarterly Almanac, 1969*, p. 583.
14. Richard Cyert and James March, *A Behavioral Theory of the Firm*, pp. 120–122.
15. Jonathan Bendor and Terry M. Moe, "An Adaptive Model of Bureaucratic Politics," pp. 755–774.
16. Quoted in *Congressional Quarterly Almanac, 1972*, p. 142.
17. They were the responsibilities under the Federal Hazardous Substances Act, the Poison Prevention Packaging Act, the Flammable Fabrics Act, and the Refrigerator Safety Act. *Congressional Quarterly Almanac, 1972*, p. 142.
18. *National Journal*, June 12, 1971, pp. 1266–1274.
19. Ibid., p. 1273.

20. U.S. Congress, Senate Committee on Labor and Public Welfare, Subcommittee on Health, *Hearings on Cosmetic Safety Act of 1974*, p. 62.

21. Ibid., p. 66.

22. *Congressional Quarterly Almanac, 1969* and *1971*.

23. *Congressional Quarterly Almanac, 1975*, p. 585.

24. Ibid., p. 585.

25. Of course, such an attitude would be wise even if the agency did not really support them, since it shows a willingness to cooperate as well as to protect the health and safety of the public.

26. Side effects of drugs are justified by the severity of the illnesses they are supposed to ameliorate.

27. Interview with FDA official.

28. This is consistent with the notion of problemistic search outlined by Cyert and March, *A Behavioral Theory of the Firm*.

29. U.S. Congress, House Committee on Interstate and Foreign Commerce, Subcommittee on Public Health and the Environment, *Hearings on FDA Oversight—Food Inspection*.

30. U.S. Congress, House Committee on Interstate and Foreign Commerce, Subcommittee on Public Health and the Environment, *Hearings on Food Labelling and Food Inspection*.

31. Alfred Marcus, "Environmental Protection Agency," in Wilson, *The Politics of Regulation*, p. 267.

32. Interview with FDA official.

33. Staff members said the Senate Labor and Human Resources Committee pursued very little oversight after 1981 because the chairman, Senator Hatch, was a loyal supporter of the Reagan Administration and did not want to embarrass it.

34. Interview with FDA official.

35. U.S. Congress, House Committee on Interstate and Foreign Commerce, Subcommittee on Oversight and Investigations, *Medical Devices Regulation: The FDA's Neglected Child*, pp. 1–5.

36. Interview with FDA official.

37. Ibid.

38. In 1974 the provision was an amendment to a health manpower program; the bill died.

39. The House passed such a bill; the Senate did not.

40. *Congressional Quarterly Almanac, 1972*, p. 731.

41. Interview with FDA official.

42. Environmental Defense Fund and Robert H. Boyle, *Malignant Neglect*, p. 30.

43. Interview with FDA official.

44. Interview with FDA official.

45. Interview with FDA official.

46. Interview with FDA official.

47. Interview with staff member.

48. Interview with FDA official.

49. Interview with FDA official.

50. Interview with FDA official.

51. Interview with FDA official.

5

The Social and Rehabilitation Service

> While you're living in your mansion,
> you don't know what hard times mean.
> Poor working man's wife is starving;
> your wife is living like a queen.
> —Bessie Smith, *Poor Man's Blues*

Created by a departmental reorganization in 1967, the Social and Rehabilitation Service (SRS) in the Department of Health, Education, and Welfare (HEW) brought together a broad variety of programs that provided services to the disadvantaged. Although some of these programs were large and well known, the SRS itself was never well established or widely recognized. In 1977, during the early years of the Carter Administration, the SRS was organized out of existence as the programs it administered were placed in different agencies throughout the department.

Coordinating and organizing social welfare and social service programs are always problematic because politicians and administrators have to decide if they want to arrange programs by function or beneficiary. In 1967, the Johnson Administration rejected the organizational choice of placing programs with the same function—such as Medicare and Medicaid—in one agency and embraced an organization structured according to the intended beneficiaries. Following this reasoning, the SRS was given responsibility for programs serving the poor, the elderly, and the disabled. This arrangement was supposed to help to coordinate different services that would often be received by the same individuals and create an agency with a strong ideological mission: to help America's disadvantaged.

The SRS administered two major transfer programs that served the poor, Aid to Families with Dependent Children (AFDC) and Medicaid. The Social Services Grant Program, a program that allowed states to provide an array of services to individuals on welfare, was also the SRS's responsibility.

The agency also administered programs providing services for the elderly, the disabled, and youth, including vocational rehabilitation, the Older Americans Act, and the prevention of juvenile delinquency. Unlike AFDC and Medicaid, these programs were not means-tested. They were not targeted specifically at low-income individuals, although many of the individuals participating in them were poor. The juxtaposition of these programs with the transfer programs for the poor created many problems for the SRS during its short tenure.

The programs within the SRS relied heavily on state administration. AFDC and Medicaid are jointly implemented by the states and the federal government. The states make many important decisions about eligibility for the programs and the kinds of services provided. These joint arrangements complicate the administration of any program, not only because they limit the authority of the federal agency and increase the number of interests involved, but also because they increase the number of relationships among those interests. The involvement of the states complicated the interactions between the congressional agencies and the SRS; the states were not just another interest group but important government entities in their own right.

The programs administered by the SRS were redistributive policies. Because these raise major ideological questions, subgovernment analysis predicts that policy making will be done primarily by the president and congressional leaders. Major decisions will not be left to the agency and the congressional committees. To a limited extent, this prediction holds true for the SRS. Congressional committees, but not the SRS, were involved in discussions about revamping the welfare programs and adopting national health insurance that dominated the domestic policy agenda during the Nixon presidency.

This approach, however, misses important interactions between the SRS and the congressional committees that shaped the programs administered by the agency. As illustrated by Table 5.1, floor discussions revolving around SRS's programs were infrequent; however, the com-

Table 5.1

Number of Roll-Call Votes on Programs Administered by the Social and Rehabilitation Service in the House and Senate, 1961 to 1977

Year	House	Senate
1967	0	4
1968	0	2
1969	1	0
1970	2	5
1971	4	2
1972	1	6
1973	4	3
1974	2	1
1975	0	0
1976	0	0
1977	1	2

Source: Roll-call votes were collected from the *Congressional Quarterly Almanac,* volumes dated from 1967 to 1977. Votes needed a ten-percent dissent rate, the standard rate for roll-call analysis, to be counted.

mittees and the agency often debated critical aspects of these programs. The relationships between the agency and the committees are consistent with the policy model but not the self-interest model. Conflict rose and fell as the committees and the agency pushed forward with their own views of the programs. Many disputes centered on the discretion of the agency, and the committees often criticized the agency's implementation of its programs. The disputes between the SRS and the committees were very similar to those encountered by the other agencies.

Like the other agencies, the SRS found it difficult to convince Congress to follow its lead in these policy debates. The committees used oversight hearings, frequent authorizations, and regulations to shape the programs to meet their preferences rather than those of the agency. The SRS had limited strategies and few resources to combat the legislature's arsenal. All four agencies struggled with the difficulties of creating political support, but the problems of the SRS were exacerbated by the fact that it was never well established. Many of the programs it administered had long histories, but the idea that these programs should be affiliated with each other was new and never quite got off the ground. Questions about the nature of the programs plagued the SRS and were resolved only by its dissolution in 1977.

In 1977 the SRS was quietly reorganized out of existence when the Carter Administration decided to emphasize function rather than beneficiaries. Medicaid was combined with Medicare to form the new Health Care Finance Administration. AFDC and the Social Services Grant Program were transferred to the Social Security Administration, the agency responsible for income maintenance programs.

The agency's interactions with two sets of committees are important. The House Education and Labor Committee and the Senate Labor and Public Welfare Committee had jurisdiction over many of the poverty programs. The House Ways and Means and Senate Finance Committees' jurisdiction over the Social Security Act meant that they too dealt with many of these programs. This chapter covers the administrative-legislative interactions over the lifetime of the SRS, 1967 to 1977.

The Social Services Grant Program

Disputes over the Social Services Grant Program centered around both its scope and its beneficiaries. Established in 1956 under the Social Security Act, the program provided federal matching funds to states to enable them to provide a range of services to individuals receiving public assistance. Those services could include such things as family planning, child care, and drug abuse counseling. When the Department of Health, Education, and Welfare and the Congress attempted to limit the program, the agency reacted in a predictable manner; it resisted initial efforts to restrict the federal government's contribution. However, the enactment of a legislative lid on the authorization did not end the conflict between the agency and the committees. When the agency lost the battle over closing the authorization, it wanted the services to be directed at the most disadvantaged individuals. The committees balked when the agency pushed for more restrictive guidelines on the purchase of services. In this second dispute over social services, the debate centered not on the scope of the program but on its goals and its beneficiaries. Consistent with the policy model, the agency and the committees responded to different pressures, and conflict developed as they presented different perspectives on these questions of program operation.

The first dispute centered on closing the open-ended authorization for the federal grant program for social services. States decided how much money they wanted to spend on social services, and the federal government matched their expenditures. Because the program was open-ended, the federal government had no control over how much it spent. It was required to match whatever effort came from the states. Although the authorization had always been open, changes in the law in the 1950s and 1960s made the program more attractive to the states and committed more funds from the federal government. Amendments to the Social Security Act between 1956 and 1967 liberalized the definition of social services. In 1967 federal matching for state social services was raised to seventy-five percent. Because this rate was higher than that of other matching grant programs, states had an incentive to switch activities from other programs to social services. The states, starting with California and then Illinois, took advantage of these provisions to fund a whole host of activities that did not actually meet the intention of the program.[1]

Initially, the federal government stimulated the expansion of the grant program. The SRS encouraged the use of social services by the state welfare departments. Changes in leadership during the Nixon Administration continued, and probably even exacerbated, this expansion. The new administration wanted to increase the role of generalists rather than that of program specialists,[2] and emphasizing broad social services over more specific and narrow programs was one way to do so.[3] A new subdivision of SRS, the Community Services Administration (CSA), was created in 1969 to administer the social services program. The CSA continued to advance social services rather than try to restrain their use.[4] In two years, from fiscal 1969 to fiscal 1971, spending on social services more than doubled, jumping to $750 million from $354 million.[5]

This rapid increase in spending indicated a problem, but it merely hinted at the growth that followed. Only a few states had already taken advantage of the loophole; however, when the SRS wrote what was supposedly a clarifying memorandum, it alerted the other states to the possibility of using social services to fund a wide variety of activities. When $1.6 billion was spent on social services in fiscal 1972 and $2.1 billion was estimated for fiscal 1973, pressures to close the authorization develcped.[6]

The first move to do this came from HEW. The administration tried unsuccessfully in 1970 and 1971 to limit the matching grants through appropriations.[7] After that approach failed, the HEW resorted to an administrative solution. It directed the agency to write restrictive regulations that outlined program goals and developed program and fiscal controls. The SRS was not very sympathetic with the department's request. According to James Bax, the head of the subdivision administering the grant program, these expenditures were not excessive. "The recent expansion has increased the daily per person expenditure for services from about $.16 to $.28," he said. "That's not enough for an RC and a moon pie."[8] Rather than scaling down the program, the regulations proposed by the SRS would have created some new required services in addition to continuing and sometimes increasing federal financing. After receiving regulations that did the opposite of what was intended, the department rejected them.[9]

The next approach was a legislative solution. Although the agency had frustrated the attempt at restrictive regulations, it could do nothing to stop the congressional committees once they decided to act. The House Ways and Means and Senate Finance committees had no problem finding support for a ceiling on authorizations; the only dilemma they faced was trying to find a bill to which they could attach the limits. Initially, both included ceilings on the expenditures in the administration's welfare reform bill in 1972. But the bill did not move quickly because it was embroiled in controversy. (Ultimately it did not pass.) A concurrent effort by the Appropriations committees failed in conference as the conferees responded to the opposition of state governors, welfare directors, and county officials. Finally, the Senate Finance and House Ways and Means committees included a ceiling of $2.5 billion in the General Revenue Sharing Act. The general revenue sharing bill was an appropriate mechanism to force the states to accept the ceiling because the committees had something to trade with the states. In order to reduce state opposition to the ceiling, the committees swapped unlimited social services funds for fiscal relief.[10]

The SRS did not support the brake on its program imposed by the authorizing committees. The funds provided for social services did not seem excessive to the agency, especially when one considered how much was actually spent per person. Yet the agency could not prevent the committees from acting. Like the Bureau of Reclamation, the Bureau of Indian Affairs, and the Food and Drug Administration, the SRS had few strategies to try to convince the committees that its policy should be advanced. The program had already been expanded to broaden the range of benefits. This sparked state interest in the program, providing the SRS with a constituent group to lobby for it. Yet even state officials could not convince Congress to maintain the open-ended authorization. Alarmed by the rapid increase in federal funding from 1969 to 1972, the committees clearly felt that too much money was being spent. The agency tried another approach, convincing the committees that the expenditure was justified, but it was unable to persuade Congress of the merits of the program.

Once the legislature decided that the grant program would have a ceiling, the dispute over the size of the program was resolved. However, a change in advocacy roles led to another dispute over the discretion of the SRS. In the second dispute over the social services program, the agency tried to restrict the program while the committees pressed for broader regulations. Consistent with the policy model, each body pushed for a program that would meet its own policy objectives.

After the committees placed a ceiling on the program, they instructed the SRS to develop regulations on the purchase of services. The agency's guidelines, presented to the committees in 1973, granted more control to the federal government over what services could and could not be financed by the matching grant program. When the program was open-ended, the agency felt it did not need to tighten up on the services the states could provide. But facing a more limited program, the SRS wanted the states to direct the program toward the most disadvantaged individuals.

Consensus within the agency on the strictness of the regulations did not arise without a debate. The new commissioner of the SRS, James Dwight, had several tiffs with the career civil servants as he tried to tighten up the agency's administration:

> For about a year, there was an article about Dwight every day in the *Federal Times* that went on about his management excesses. In the final analysis the senior people in the Community Services Administration were pretty comfortable with the regulations. Five or six people helped write them. They were put on the table and discussed. Everyone had their day in court, so to speak. That was after two years of pitched camp.[11]

The career civil servants responded more slowly to the need to target the program and had to be persuaded by the agency's top officials to accept the new restrictions. This process was complicated by the Nixon

Administration's problems with management in the early 1970s. Eventually, a consensus was reached, and the agency presented the regulations to the committees without having a split among its personnel.

The regulations were vigorously opposed by almost everyone outside of HEW. In response to protests from a number of legislators, the Senate Finance and the House Ways and Means committees postponed the effective date of the regulations twice, once until January 1974, and a year later until January 1975, to give the legislature time to evaluate the regulations. The Senate Finance Committee reported that the new regulations were "so far out of step with the clear requirements of the statute and with congressional intent" that the Congress needed to decide "what kinds of policies should be incorporated in law rather than left for regulatory interpretation."[12] The committees decided they could not rely on the SRS to develop regulations that would meet congressional aims. They wrote the regulations themselves. In 1974 the committees devised, and Congress adopted, guidelines which established national goals and standards but gave the states considerable leeway in deciding which social service programs they would provide.[13]

This later dispute over the Social Services Grant Program focused not on the scope of the program nor the authority of the agency but on whose goals should be advanced and which beneficiaries should be served. As in the policy model, the agency and the committees responded to different factors in formulating their policy goals. Once the SRS was told that the funds for the grant program would be limited, the agency wrote regulations that tightened up the worst abuses of the program. It emphasized national goals and standards and tried to encourage states to provide services to the most disadvantaged by limiting the types of services they could provide. This approach was a shift from the earlier tendency to encourage an expansion of the program, but it was a shift that was required by the restricted resources the program now received.

The committees developed a different perspective on the regulations as they responded to the preferences of constituents and state governments that wanted to maintain some of the discretion they had when they had been able to use the grant program for almost any service they wanted to provide. The committees pushed the agency to broaden the grant program so that states would have more freedom to fund the services they preferred. The committees wanted to limit federal funding yet retain the broad program that existed under the earlier open-ended authorization.

A recurrent problem in grant programs is whether national or state aims should be emphasized. In this case, the committees disagreed with the agency over whose goals should be advanced. The committees did not grant the agency the discretion to decide how to target the program. Rather, they closely scrutinized the agency's proposal. By writing the regulations themselves, they restricted the authority of the SRS.

Disputes over Program Beneficiaries

Social welfare programs can provide benefits to a vast array of individuals. A critical issue in these programs is deciding who should be eligible for services and within these guidelines what groups should have the highest priority for services. Although the SRS was supposed to administer programs for the disadvantaged, no overarching policy on eligibility tied the programs together. Because Congress formulated no such policy, and the SRS did not develop one over time, questions about who should be served dominated many of the disputes between the SRS and its congressional committees.

The first dispute, over priorities for service in vocational rehabilitation, centered on tightening up the discretion of the agency. Responding to complaints from constituents, the committees wanted the program to give priority to the most severely disabled individuals. Concerned with maintaining a mission it felt it could justify and protect, the agency resisted these efforts to target the most disabled. Like the Food and Drug Administration when it opposed new tasks in the 1970s and fought off special exemptions to the Delaney clause, the SRS was trying to protect the integrity of the program.

When the House Education and Labor and Senate Labor and Public Welfare committees reauthorized the Vocational Rehabilitation Division in 1973, they were anxious about service delivery. The members wanted the division to shift its emphasis so that more persons with severe disabilities would be served.[14] Vocational Rehabilitation, they felt, focused on those cases that could be easily and quickly resolved, thus boosting the number of successful rehabilitations completed by the agency. Although HEW officials responded to the criticisms by vowing that they would redirect the program and increase the targets for the percentage of severely disabled persons served, legislators were not satisfied with such promises. The committees wanted specific statutory references to emphasize that priority should be given to severely disabled individuals.

The reluctance of the Vocational Rehabilitation Division of SRS to accept such changes stemmed from the fact that they would alter the mission of the program. As the policy model predicts, the agency was concerned with protecting the integrity of the programs it administered. The goal of the program had always been employment of rehabilitated individuals. If severely disabled persons became a more significant clientele, employment could no longer be so strongly emphasized. It was the benefits from the employment of disabled persons that the Vocational Rehabilitation Division used to show the advantages and achievements of its program. In the Senate Committee report, for example, the program was justified as a worthwhile investment of the federal government because of the money saved and the very high benefit–cost ratio.[15] If the creaming of the least disabled individuals were stopped, the money saved and the benefit–cost ratio would decline, thus jeopardizing the justification for the program. Although the change might seem minor, the bureaucrats were reluctant to change their approach because they believed it was a fundamental shift in the mission of the program.

Like the Social Services Program, the SRS could not prevent the committees from changing Vocational Rehabilitation. In 1973 the reauthorized program gave priority to the most severely disabled individuals. The law did not earmark funds or set targets, but it specified that state rehabilitation agencies had to serve the most severely disabled first.[16] The committees recognized that this priority would change the type of services provided by downplaying employment and emphasizing functional skills.

In additional debates over priorities, the committees again resorted to their legislative authority in order to gain agency compliance with congressional wishes. This time, though, the committees decided to remove two divisions, the Administration on Aging and the Rehabilitation Services Administration, from the jurisdiction of the SRS. In these incidents, the committees clashed with the Nixon Administration, which opposed the transfers, but not the SRS. The agency did not care that the programs were removed from its turf. It developed no sense that its programs should be interdependent; they remained separate entities which competed against each other for status and resources.

Because the SRS lacked a policy on who was disadvantaged, it never developed a sense of what programs should fit together in order to best serve that group. In fact, subdivisions within the agency tried not to be labeled as programs for the disadvantaged, and an easy way to accomplish that was to get out of the SRS.

Two divisions of the Social and Rehabilitation Service were transferred by Congress out of the agency to the Office of the Secretary of Health, Education, and Welfare in 1973 and 1974. In making these changes the committee members responded to complaints from the clientele of these programs that they were not receiving enough attention and that they did not like being associated with welfare programs. No particular problem with service delivery captured the legislators' attention, nor were they reacting to a general ideological concern about social welfare programs. Rather they responded to the demands of clientele who were vying with other groups for resources and priorities and felt the placement of these programs in the SRS hindered their competitive position.

In 1973, following the recommendations of the Senate Labor and Public Welfare and the House Education and Labor committees, Congress removed the Administration on Aging from the SRS. The action represented support for the programs but opposition to their administration. The committees felt that these programs had not been given enough attention and were buried under HEW hierarchical layers, contrary to their interpretation that the 1965 statute authorizing the programs mandated high visibility. The pattern in both the Johnson and Nixon administrations, according to Representative John Brademas (D–IN), was:

> to downgrade, to cripple, to weaken, to diminish the authority of the Commissioner. The crippling reached a point where we used to feel sorry for our good friend John Martin [the Commissioner of the Administration on Aging]. Everyday he came in and he had lost more authority and program control until, finally, he was so far down in the bureaucratic hierarchy that he had almost no program money.[17]

The legislative action did not seem to have been stimulated by a particular problem. Although members referred frequently to the effectiveness of the commissioner being jeopardized, they did not discuss a specific problem or gap in service delivery. The major problem seemed to be the association of the program with services for the poor. A common complaint was that the dominant programs in SRS were income maintenance programs and that it was a "welfare agency." Because the Older Americans program was not supposed to be a welfare program, it should not have been placed alongside AFDC and Medicaid.[18]

Another similar situation developed at the same time with a different subunit of SRS, the Rehabilitation Services Administration. In 1973 the same committees first moved to leave the rehabilitation program within the SRS, but they gave it statutory authority and specified that only the commissioner of the Rehabilitation Services Administration could administer the program. The following year, after continued complaints, the division was moved out of SRS entirely and placed in the Office of the Secretary of HEW.

Again, the legislators' concern was the visibility of the program and its juxtaposition with welfare programs.[19] The committees were responding to clientele grievances. According to one witness at a congressional hearing, the program, after being placed in SRS, was "sort of like a drowning man who is trying to swim to shore with four or five other people around his neck."[20] Rehabilitation services could not hold up other programs like AFDC that had little constituency support and virtually no organizational vitality.

The Nixon Administration opposed both of these transfers because they upset the systematic and orderly management of social welfare programs it was trying to achieve. Yet the SRS did not really care that the Administration on Aging was transferred out of its jurisdiction. A top level administrator in SRS said, "It was a non-issue, nobody cared. I didn't care, people from SRS weren't coming in to me and saying this is awful."[21] Nor was there great concern about the transfer of the Rehabilitation Services Administration.

This absence of conflict fits with the policy model but not the self-interest model. SRS officials did not behave like budget-maximizing bureaucrats trying to protect their turf when they acquiesced to the transfers. From the policy perspective of the SRS, the transfers were irrelevant. The agency had not developed any organizational integrity, any sense that the various units should fit together or that their fates were somehow related. Because the units were separated and distinguished from each other, the removal of one division did not really matter; it had no effect on the other sections of the agency. The two subdivisions of the SRS, however, thought differently. The Administration on Aging and the Rehabilitation Services Administration supported the transfers for policy reasons. They believed their association with the means-tested programs jeopardized their standing, and that the changes illustrated the importance the committees placed on their programs.

The Social and Rehabilitation Service did not develop any organizational integrity for two reasons. A primary factor was the unwillingness of those affiliated with programs that did not solely serve the poor to be identified with means-tested programs. Because welfare has a pejorative connotation, it is not surprising that clientele felt an association with AFDC and Medicaid would hurt the standing of aging and rehabilitation programs. Each division was trying to build support to maintain its programs, but that led to no overall strategy that would benefit the agency as a whole. Secondly, coordinating these various programs in the SRS required changes at the state level that were often opposed by program implementors. According to one SRS official, the debate over the placement of rehabilitation services was sparked by an agency move to alter the way state services were organized. This began when James Dwight, the head of SRS, granted a waiver to Arizona that altered existing bureaucratic structure, and the rehabilitation services did not like it because

> it was a change, and a change they never had to deal with before. When SRS was set up, Switzer [Mary Switzer, the first head of the agency] had been the head of rehab for like forever, and they made sure that Switzer was part of SRS. We changed that by changing one of the guiding rules—that the state vocational rehab director is the guru. We undercut their turf.[22]

The waiver meant that the SRS granted more authority to program generalists at the state level and less authority to program specialists. Uniting the SRS to coordinate all of these programs would have been extremely difficult because further changes in the relative power of the generalists and specialists would have been required. Altering the organizational and management structures at the state level was not impossible, but the SRS did not have the time or the energy to effect those changes. Without them, it was difficult for the agency to create any overarching policy that tied the disparate subdivisions together.

Questions of Management

Like the Food and Drug Administration and the Bureau of Indian Affairs, the SRS was frequently criticized by congressional committees. As demonstrated by the disputes over social services, rehabilitation, and programs for the aging, much of this criticism occurred through the routine authorization of programs. But the committees also conducted oversight hearings, especially when they wanted to investigate program implementation in hopes of cutting administrative costs.

Periodic authorization of programs was a convenient way for the committees to set goals and deadlines for program improvement. Often the committees would authorize a program for only a year or two, warning the agency that it expected to see improvements before the next set of hearings. Vocational rehabilitation was authorized in 1968, 1973, and 1974. The Juvenile Delinquency Prevention and Control Act of 1968 was reauthorized in 1971 but only for one year. Annoyed with the lack of progress in implementing the program, the House Education and Labor Committee shortened the authorization period. It directed the SRS to use the year to coordinate and improve the administration of the act.[23] The Early and Periodic Screening, Diagnostic, and Treatment Program, a section of Medicaid aimed at children, was a program the SRS could not get off the ground. Although it was initially authorized in 1967, the SRS still had not issued any regulations five years later. In order to push the agency along, the committees established a deadline for guidelines in 1972.[24]

The committees also used general oversight hearings to check up on the implementation of programs. The House Ways and Means and the Senate Finance committees were tied up with welfare reform from 1969 through 1972. After the reform fell through, the committees concentrated on tightening the administration of AFDC. The House Ways and Means Committee investigated HEW's efforts to reduce costs and error rates in the means-tested program in 1975 and 1976.[25]

It was Medicaid, though, that received most of the oversight attention from the committees. During the time that SRS was responsible for Medicaid, both the House Ways and Means and the Senate Finance committees checked regulations, oversaw management practices, and pushed for controls on cost and utilization. Congress had ignored the details of the program when it was adopted in 1965; most of its attention was focused on Medicare, an insurance program for the elderly with relatively clear provisions for eligibility and benefits. Although Congress had neglected to define the shape or scope of Medicaid when it was authorized, this neglect quickly ended once HEW started implementing the program.

The committees' actions were sparked by the realization that the Medicaid program would be much larger than anticipated. The first inkling of the size of the program came in 1966 when New York submitted its Medicaid plan for approval. The plan required the federal government to provide $145 million more in matching funds than the state had received under Kerr–Mills, a federal program adopted in 1960 that provided grants to states to help provide medical care for the indigent elderly, yet HEW had estimated the additional cost of the program nationwide at $155 million.[26] Obviously, something had to be changed.

The low estimates of the federal cost of the program stemmed from the fact that eligibility for Medicaid was set by the states within guidelines established by the federal government. The guidelines allowed the states to provide Medicaid to the "medically needy," those individuals who were not eligible for categorical relief programs but were too poor to pay for their own health care. The federal government gave the states considerable leeway in deciding who was "medically needy," and they underestimated the number of persons who would fit this category.

The committees' involvement in overseeing Medicaid began in 1967, the same year that SRS received responsibility for the program. The committees' goal was to tighten up the program. According to the House Ways and Means report, the committees had never intended that the federal government would subsidize the medical care of a large portion of population with moderate incomes.[27] Through amendments to the Social Security Act, the committees limited the eligibility of the medically needy and relaxed some of the standards for state services.[28] These changes were supposed to clarify the federal government's role in Medicaid that was so vague in the initial authorization.

The 1967 amendments were not sufficient for the Senate Finance Committee. Under Senator Russell Long's (D–LA) guidance, the committee emerged as the primary watchdog of Medicaid. It continued to try to restrain the scope of the program through legislative changes in both 1968 and 1969.[29] In 1969 and 1970 the committee conducted a thorough study of both Medicaid and Medicare. The committee was primarily concerned about the action of the states and the providers of health care, but it did not ignore the federal implementation of the programs. It attacked the agency for delays and permissiveness. The staff report summarized its assessment of Medicaid's management:

> Federal officials have been lax in not seeing to it that States establish and employ effective control on utilization and costs, and States have been unwilling to assume the responsibility on their own. The Federal Medicaid administrators have not provided States with the expert assistance necessary to establish and implement proper controls. Also, they have not developed mechanisms for coordination and communication among the States about methods of identifying and solving Medicaid problems.[30]

As the studies of the other three agencies demonstrate, using legislation to steer programs is not unusual for a congressional committee. Neither is the use of legislative oversight. However, the Senate Finance Committee used its authority in a somewhat unusual way because it conducted the most comprehensive study of Medicaid and Medicare of its time in 1969. Rather than wait for the agency to study the programs, the committee staff investigated program usage and costs. The hearings were an opportunity for Long and his assistants to tell the administration and other senators what was happening with the two health care programs.

The Medical Services Administration (MSA), the division of SRS responsible for Medicaid, was too small and weak to have much of a response to the committees' actions. In 1965 the division had only twenty-three employees; by 1969 that number had risen only to seventy-six positions in the national office.[31] Although the MSA was unable to act, the department was encouraged by the Senate Committee's study to shore up the division. After a task force studied the program, a new commissioner was appointed, staff positions were added, and the division was reorganized.[32]

The committees did not stop regulating Medicaid after the MSA was rejuvenated. They continued to monitor the progress of the program through hearings and legislative changes. For example, Professional Standards Review Organizations, established in 1972 with the hope that health care professionals could review and thus control health care costs, were investigated in the Ninety-fourth Congress. Again, the legislators prodded the SRS to move more quickly in implementing the program.

The committees' concern with criticism of agency management is consistent with the policy model but not the self-interest model. The SRS faced frequent congressional criticism, as both sets of committees kept watch over its implementation of programs. The committees did not simply hold hearings investigating agency decisions; they used a variety of legislative tools such as goals, deadlines, and periodic authorizations to alter the way the SRS administered its programs.

Concluding Thoughts

Even though the SRS administered redistributive policy, the congressional committees played integral roles in shaping its programs. Because the subgovernment variant of the self-interest model claims that redistributive policies will be decided on the floor of the House and Senate chambers, it provides little guidance in understanding the interactions between the SRS and its congressional committees. The policy model, however, provides a rich set of insights into these relationships.

Consistent with the policy model, the SRS clashed frequently with its congressional committees as the two groups developed different views of desirable public policy. A dispute over the scope of the agency's programs developed when the agency and the committees clashed over the size of the Social Services Grant Program, one of the agency's major programs. Conflicts over the way in which the agency exercised its authority emerged several times, encompassing the Social Services Grant Program as well as Vocational Rehabilitation. In these debates, the committees reduced the discretion of the agency in order to shift the focus of the programs. Also, the committees often criticized the agency's management, lamenting the low priority given to programs and the delays in implementing them.

Although the SRS resisted the limitation of the Social Services Program, it did not object to the removal of the Rehabilitation Services Administration or the Administration on Aging. The absence of conflict in both of these cases can be explained by the policy model but not by the self-interest model. Because the agency had no overarching policy tying the disparate subdivisions together, the organizational changes made little difference to the SRS, even though they removed programs from its purview.

Like the other agencies, the SRS rarely won when it clashed with Congress. There was little it could do to try to convince the committees that its perspective was correct. The strategy of expanding a program or targeting benefits was not helpful when the congressional committees had already decided it needed to be limited. Constituents could lobby to maintain programs, but they did not always share the same objectives as the agency. Procrastination, successfully used by the Bureau of Indian Affairs during the period of termination, was not effective when the committees used periodic authorizations to check up on progress in implementing programs. The SRS was unable to counteract the committees' persistent use of a variety of control devices to shape the programs to meet their own preferences.

Notes

1. A complete description of the development of the states' use of this grant program and the federal government's responses to the loophole is outlined in *Uncontrollable Spending in Social Service Grants* by Martha Derthick.

2. Ibid., pp. 35–37.

3. Ibid., p. 39.

4. Ibid., p. 37.

5. *National Journal*, June 17, 1972, p. 1007.

6. Ibid., p. 1007.

7. *National Journal*, January 29, 1972, p. 179.

8. Ibid., p. 1014.

9. *National Journal*, June 17, 1972, pp. 1007–1014.

10. Derthick, *Uncontrollable Spending in Social Service Grants*, p. 76.

11. Interview with SRS official.

12. U.S. Congress, Senate Committee on Finance, S Report 93–249, p. 39.

13. *Congressional Quarterly Almanac, 1974*, p. 505.

14. U.S. Congress, House Committee on Education and Labor, H Report 93–244, p. 6.

15. U.S. Congress, Senate Committee on Labor and Public Welfare, S Report 93–218, p.18.

16. *Congressional Quarterly Almanac, 1973*, p. 557.

17. U.S. Congress, House Committee on Education and Labor, Select Subcommittee on Education, *Hearings to Amend the Older Americans Act of 1965*, p. 49.

18. Testimony of Harry Walker, in U.S. Congress, House Committee on Education and Labor, Select Subcommittee on Education, *Oversight Hearings on Older Americans*, pp. 13–14.

19. U.S. Congress, Senate Committee on Labor and Public Welfare, S Report 93–1139, p. 19.

20. Testimony of Dr. Howard Rusk, Director of the Institute for Rehabilitative Medicine, in U.S. Congress, Senate Committee on Labor and Public Welfare,

Subcommittee on the Handicapped, *Hearings*, p. 691.

21. Interview with SRS administrator.

22. Interview with SRS official.

23. *Congressional Quarterly Almanac, 1971*, p. 781; and U.S. Congress, House Committee on Education and Labor, H Report 92–282, p. 3.

24. *National Journal*, June 29, 1974, pp. 969–974.

25. U.S. Congress, House Committee on Ways and Means, Subcommittee on Oversight, *Hearings on AFDC Quality Control Program*; and U.S. Congress, House Committee on Ways and Means, Subcommittee on Oversight, *Hearings on HEW Efforts to Reduce Errors in Welfare Programs*.

26. Robert Stevens and Rosemary Stevens, *Welfare Medicine in America*, p. 95.

27. *Congressional Quarterly Almanac, 1967*, p. 903.

28. Ibid., p. 895.

29. The 1968 amendment, added to a House-passed tax bill, would have reduced payments by the federal government to persons not eligible for public welfare. But it was later deleted by Senator Long after a threat from liberal senators to filibuster the bill. *Congressional Quarterly Almanac, 1968*, p. 633. In 1969 Long was more successful. Attached to an import duty on shoe lathes, his provision permitted states to cut back certain Medicaid services and postponed the deadline when states would be required to establish a comprehensive program. *Congressional Quarterly Almanac, 1969*, p. 201.

30. U.S. Congress, Senate Committee on Finance, *Hearings on Medicare and Medicaid*, p. 32.

31. Stevens and Stevens, *Welfare Medicine in America*, pp. 78, 114.

32. Ibid., pp. 237–241.

6

Conclusions

The Constitution of the United States encourages conflict among the branches of the national government in order to regulate the exercise of power. The Founders intended the separate institutions with independent sources of authority to clash over policy making. But the value of conflict among bureaucrats and politicians is more ambiguous than disputes between institutions because the authority of administrators is delegated to them by elected officials. Conflict between these two groups of decision makers appears illegitimate when it is seen as indicating that administrators are not following the wishes of elected officials. Yet conflict could result in better policy decisions if it arises from the inclusion of a broad variety of interests in the policy process. A system that fosters consensus between administrators and elected officials could also be a system in which important policy goals and consequences are ignored.

In order to shed light on these issues, this book examined the dynamics of conflict between four agencies and their congressional committees. The findings of this study suggest that we should not try to reduce or eliminate conflict between bureaucrats and legislators, even though we may want a system in which disputes are manageable and the legislature has the upper hand in controlling them. Conflict does not automatically indicate that legislative prescriptions are flagrantly ignored by a willful bureaucracy. Often it suggests that the bureaucracy can make significant and meaningful contributions to the policy process, contributions that will not necessarily come from other policy makers. Just as we view conflict among the president, the Congress, and the judiciary as desirable, so can we similarly see conflict between bureaucrats and legislators.

Theories of Conflict

Chapter One developed two models with fundamentally different assumptions—the self-interest model and the policy model—that lead to distinct hypotheses about the nature and extent of conflict between agencies and congressional committees. Then, by reconstructing the legislative histories of four agencies—the Bureau of Reclamation, the Bureau of Indian Affairs, the Food and Drug Administration, and the Social and Rehabilitation Service—from 1961 to 1984, we tested the hypotheses of the two models. As Chapters Two through Five indicate, the patterns of conflict and consensus fit the policy model. The self-interest model provides little understanding of the relationships between the agencies and committees because it cannot account for their interactions.

In the self-interest model, consensus arises as each actor pursues his or her self-interest. Legislators want to be reelected, bureaucrats want to maximize their budgets, and voters want to maximize their net benefits. To meet their respective goals, both legislators and administrators agree that government programs should be expanded. Once a program is adopted, legislators have little incentive to supervise the agency's actions; they grant the agency broad discretion to implement the program, choosing to devote their scarce resources to other activities that seem to have a more direct reelection payoff.

The subgovernment variant is a more sophisticated adaptation of the self-interest model. Asserting that the policy determines the politics, the subgovernment variant argues that consensual interactions will be found in distributive policies. In regulatory and redistributive policies, subgovernments lose power to macropolitical actors such as the president, the political parties, and congressional leaders. Because these policies are addressed by a broader array of decision makers, debates are more partisan, more ideological, and thus more conflictual.

Because the policy model makes different assumptions about the motivation of the actors, it draws a different picture of the relationships between agencies and committees. In the policy model both bureaucrats and legislators have policy goals. Legislators, especially those who hold committee leadership positions, have personal, ideological, and institutional incentives not only to advance certain policies but also to ensure that bureaucratic actions are consistent with those policies. Even though they respect the policy-making responsibility of the legislature, agencies develop their own policy views as they react to demands of clientele, directives of other institutions such as the judiciary, previous legislative guidelines, and their past experience with a program.

The nature of the relationships between the four agencies studied and their congressional committees—the patterns of conflict and consensus—fit with the policy model but not the self-interest model. First, all four agencies collided with congressional committees, even though they administered very different types of policies. This was true even for the agency that administered distributive policy: the Bureau of Reclamation, an agency with a reputation for extensive congressional support, fought intensely with the committees over several of its projects. This is consistent with the policy model, in which conflict is inevitable because policy goals diverge, but not with the self-interest model, which predicts that consensus would be the norm and conflict would be rare. None of the agencies were able to avoid disputes with their authorizing committees. The agencies were not assured of congressional endorsement of all of the programs and activities they pursued, nor could they assume that their actions would escape congressional criticism. Similarly, the committees did not have the luxury of knowing that agencies would comply with congressional directives without the need for nudging. At least between agencies and committees, the goal of the Founders—to develop a system that encouraged conflict—was accomplished.

Second, members of subgovernments, the "insiders," played critical roles in initiating these disputes. According to the self-interest model, disputes would be raised by "outsiders" when they forced open a closed subgovernment that refused to consider opposing interests. But in the policy model, "insiders" have many reasons to address critical policy issues. Both the legislators and the bureaucrats want to promote their policy positions, and they try to persuade the other group to accept them. The aggressiveness of the committees is the best evidence to support this conclusion. The committees did not adopt a laissez-faire attitude toward the bureaus. They initiated many of the disputes by steering the direction of the policies administered by the agencies. To ensure that policies were consistent with their own preferences, they proposed new legislation, altered existing tasks, and watched the implementation of programs. Some legislators, like Representative L.H. Fountain and Senator Russell Long, set committee agendas in order to pursue policies of great interest to them. The committees were staffed with legislators who had many reasons to watch carefully the agencies' actions.

Third, conflict was not disruptive. Conflicts rose and fell. Sometimes the underlying issues were resolved, sometimes they faded away. But conflict over one issue did not lead to conflict over another issue, even when the agencies clashed with committees over fundamental policy questions. The system was the loosely knit system of the policy model. When the Interior committees and the Bureau of Indian Affairs disagreed about the overarching policy for Indian affairs, they were still able to make decisions on a number of other issues, such as continued aid for vocational education. The Bureau of Reclamation experienced intense conflicts with committees over the public provision of power and the authorization of the Central Arizona Project, yet the disputes did not fracture the subgovernment because they were not tied to other bureau programs. Even in the late 1970s and early 1980s, when the general issues of environmental degradation and resource scarcity confronted the entire reclamation program, the subgovernment was not faced with the prospects of disintegration. Contrary to the self-interest model, conflict did not force the subgovernments to adapt or face disintegration.

Fourth, questions about the scope of the agencies' authority arose frequently, even though three of the four bureaus were well established. Most disputes centered around proposals by legislators to restrict the agencies' programs. Few of these conflicts were initiated by aggressive agencies looking for new tasks; in fact, some disputes arose because the bureaus did not want to accept the additional responsibilities proposed by the legislature.

These disputes cannot be predicted by the self-interest model. In this model conflicts over scope would be rare because an agency and a committee would agree to expand the bureau's program in order to satisfy their respective goals. The subgovernment variant does not provide much additional insight. In distributive policy, questions about scope of authority would be raised only by outsiders who succeeded in breaking through the closed doors of the subgovernment. More conflict would envelope regulatory and redistributive policies, but sub-government analysis does not provide many clues as to the types of disputes that would be likely to arise. Finally, neither the self-interest model nor the subgovernment variant can account for agencies that turn down additional responsibilities and bureaus that accept policies reducing their role. Bureaucrats trying to expand their agencies in order to maximize their budgets would be acting contrary to their self-interest if they behaved in such a manner.

Disputes over scope of authority are consistent with the policy model because it recognizes that one action—expanding an agency's tasks—will not necessarily meet the goals of both legislators and bureaucrats. Because agency officials evaluate new responsibilities according to their policy goals, they will not always agree to accept new tasks; in fact, sometimes they will even agree to a reduced role for the bureau. As legislators assess administrative programs, questions about scope frequently will arise. Conflict will develop when the preferences of the committee members and agency officials do not mesh. The disputes need elaboration to demonstrate this point.

Few conflicts over authority developed because agencies initiated proposals for new programs that were opposed by the committees. When such disputes arose, the agencies' actions were not without precedent or congressional encouragement. They were consistent with past policy. The conflicts occurred because the committees responded to different forces, such as interest-group complaints and concerns of the chambers, and changed their positions on the issues.

Neither the Bureau of Indian Affairs nor the Social and Rehabilitation Service became embroiled in disputes started by administrative requests for additional authority. Two contests between the Food and Drug Administration and its committees, the confrontations over combination drugs and over vitamins and minerals, developed when the committees refused to support agency plans for additional authority. Both occurred at a time when the committees were pressing the agency to protect the consumer more aggressively. Because these particular plans aroused intense interest-group opposition, the committees retreated from their original and broad demands for more aggressive action.

Clashes between the Bureau of Reclamation and the Interior committees over the public production of power in the early 1960s and the siting of dams for the Lower Colorado River Basin Project could also be considered as agency-initiated. But both proposals were consistent with earlier policy. The Bureau of Reclamation had been given the authority to construct multipurpose projects in the 1939 reclamation law, and the agency had won an earlier fight over the construction of a dam that would affect Hell's Canyon. Although the agency must have had some idea that the projects resting on these precedents would stimulate negative responses, it also knew that the plans were consistent with the legislative directions it had been given in the past.

A major reason why few conflicts developed because of agency plans for expansion is that the bureaus were often too busy defending their current programs from attacks. Kaufman established that relatively few agencies are ever eliminated,[1] but this immortality does not necessarily mean that survival is without risk. The committees were often unhappy with the status quo and tried to reduce the scope of the agency's responsibilities. All four agencies encountered legislative plans to reduce their responsibilities, albeit in varying degrees of severity. One of the major programs of the Social and Rehabilitation Service was attacked when Congress closed the open-ended authorization for social service grants. The underpinning of the SRS was assaulted further when Congress removed the Administration on Aging and the Rehabilitation Services Administration from the agency. Even the Bureau of Reclamation faced committees that were less than enthusiastic about continuing the past reclamation program. Because of assaults from environmentalists and budget-cutters, the late 1970s and early 1980s found the agency opposing plans to restrict the reclamation program. Although the agency will continue to exist, defending its reclamation program has become a major part of its legislative activities, and its role will probably change from one of construction of water projects to operation and maintenance. The Food and Drug Administration escaped with the lightest attack; only once did legislators try to cut back the agency when some members proposed to transfer much of the FDA's authority to a new consumer agency because they were fed up with it.

The Bureau of Indian Affairs faced the severest challenges to its program by the congressional committees throughout the twenty-four years studied. The most precarious position was held by the BIA from 1954 to 1973, the period of termination, when the official policy of the United States Congress was to eliminate the need for the agency. When termination was replaced by self-determination, the position of Indian tribes on reservations was more secure, but the threat of dissolution stayed with the agency as committee members used reductions in bureau personnel as one justification for the new policy. Legislators' hostility to the renewed efforts of tribes to exercise sovereignty and treaty rights raised again the specter of termination.

Disputes also emerged because agencies refused to support legislative proposals granting them additional responsibilities. Proposals that did not mesh with current programs were viewed skeptically by the agencies. Legislative entrepreneurs pushing new programs did not always find bureaucratic acceptance. Concerned with the additional administrative burdens and the lack of discretion in the legislation, and seeing no great need for the programs, the FDA in the early 1970s refrained from supporting Senate proposals to increase the regulation of foods and cosmetics. The consensus between the FDA and the Senate committee faltered because the agency balked at accepting additional responsibilities. A similar situation did *not* develop in the 1960s, when the almost continuous congressional investigation induced problemistic search by the agency and an acceptance of legislative proposals as solutions to problems.[2]

When committees were not so active, the bureaus' reluctance to accept new tasks produced consensus rather than conflict. The aggressive promotion of particular policies by the BIA would have led to intense clashes with the Interior committees. Even when provided the opportunity to promote its expansion, the bureau accepted its restricted jurisdiction because it met its mission of serving Indians living on reservations. In the 1960s the BIA supported the involvement of other agencies in the provision of social services to tribes; in the early 1970s it refused to press for an expansion of its jurisdiction to urban Indians. Facing legislators that were probably unwilling to support expanding programs, the bureau's inactivity led to consensus with the committees.

Fifth, disputes centered not just on the scope of authority but also on the way in which the agencies exercised that authority. The committees were not content to give the agencies free rein in carrying out their responsibilities. They investigated administrative decisions about specific products, construction techniques, and the allocation of resources. Consistent with the policy model, the agencies resisted congressional intervention in the details and specifics of program implementation. Because they desired discretion, bureaus contested legislative attempts to draw strict guidelines regulating agency actions. But they pushed the members to write overarching policy that established a direction the agency could follow, and they resisted legislative decisions to grant exemptions from those general principles. The FDA's need for a legitimate, defensible policy led to the officials' reluctance to accept a case-by-case application of the Delaney clause. Concern for discretion shaped the dispute over the implementation of the medical devices law and the Senate proposals to regulate foods and cosmetics. Disputes between the SRS and its committees arose because of different views about targeting programs to specific beneficiaries.

In addition to writing detailed legislation and drawing strict guidelines, the committees tried to control the exercise of bureaucratic authority by watching the implementation of policies. Three of the four agencies encountered considerable criticism of their management by congressional committees that did not hesitate to express their opinions of administrative procedures. The agencies often had to defend their actions before legislators who had serious questions about the ways in which policies were implemented. Periodic authorizations gave the committees opportunities to investigate a program's progress. Only the Bureau of Reclamation escaped frequent complaints about its implementation of policy. Much of this oversight is consistent with Joel Aberbach's notion of oversight in a context of advocacy.[3] Legislators are often supportive of the programs themselves but very critical of the way in which bureaucrats administer those programs.

Although Aberbach discovers an increasing incidence of oversight after 1971,[4] most research on Congress does not find evidence of frequent oversight. The present study finds that oversight has a more significant role in legislative-administrative interactions owing to its definition of oversight and its research design. First, the study recognizes that oversight can occur through a variety of forums. Other research generally counts only formal oversight hearings, ignoring oversight that operates through routine authorizations.[5] Second, oversight is considered from the perspective of the agencies as well as the committees. Other studies examine oversight as a subset of congressional activity, concluding that relatively little attention is devoted to oversight when compared with other legislative activities.[6] From an agency's perspective, however, the portion of time and energy devoted to oversight by a committee does not really matter. What is important is the time and energy the *agency* has to devote to congressional oversight. Finally, this longitudinal research demonstrates that few or no congressional investigations may occur in a given year, yet over time there are often periods in which there is extensive examination of the agencies' actions. Cross-sectional studies miss these variations over time.

The policy model, through its hypotheses about the extent and emergence of conflict between authorizing committees and administrative agencies, provides a richer and more accurate understanding of these interactions. Committees aggressively used their legislative powers to advance their policy perspectives. Bureaus assessed legislative initiatives according to their missions, the desire for discretion, and the need for a defensible public policy. These policy goals diverged, making conflict between the agencies and committees inevitable. Yet these disputes did not fracture the subgovernments because they were limited to the issue at hand. Thus, the system could shift easily from consensus to conflict and back again.

Resolution of Conflict and the Negative Bias

This research has concentrated primarily on the development of conflict rather than its resolution. When considering the settlement of these disputes, one systematic bias becomes apparent, and it merits discussion. In terms of "success," or which decision-making body gets what it wants from the other, the system has a negative bias. Each group was more successful when it could satisfy its demands without requiring action by the other body. Often agencies were unable to prompt congressional action, and congressional committees had a difficult time forcing bureaus to take particular steps specified by the committees. However, the committees had the control mechanisms needed to overcome this negative bias; the bureaucracy did not.

The agencies were not successful when acting as entrepreneurs or inciting congressional action on legislative programs. The Bureau of Indian Affairs could not persuade the Interior committees to pass the Indian Resources Development Act in 1966 and 1967. Until other decision makers pressed for action, namely a president and new committee leadership interested in pursuing Indian legislation, the bureau was unable to promote congressional involvement in revising Indian policy, even though termination had been discarded as the guideline for policy making. Officials in the Food and Drug Administration wanted to see some changes made in the Delaney clause and preferred that the legislature deal with the thorny issues of accepting risks, but they could not propel the legislature into action. Members of Congress were willing to amend the laws regulating medical devices in the mid-1970s, a time when several liberal and active senators were interested in food and drug legislation, but in the early 1980s FDA administrators were not optimistic about the possibility of obtaining legislative changes they thought were necessary.

The Bureau of Reclamation is the one agency that was more likely to act as an entrepreneur and to be relatively successful at it. This is primarily because the process of adopting water projects relied on agency entrepreneurship. Proposals for new water projects were sent to the committees by the Bureau of Reclamation after initial studies about the feasibility of constructing the projects. The initial studies did not require congressional authorization, and the ideas for water projects were usually brought to the agency by local water associations and constituents.

Furthermore, the agencies were not successful at expanding their authority when they faced congressional opposition. In the few times that agencies pushed for new responsibilities in the face of congressional opposition, the committees usually prevented agency action. One of the two multipurpose water projects debated by Congress in the early 1960s was approved. Congress endorsed neither of the controversial dams accompanying the Central Arizona Project. The Food and Drug Administration was allowed to regulate vitamins and minerals but only if they were shown to be toxic. It was assumed that the products were safe rather than harmful, so the burden of proof to demonstrate otherwise fell on the agency, not the manufacturers of the products. When members complained about the proposed guidelines for combination drugs, the FDA quickly backed down and decided not to cover nonprescription drugs. If a committee chose to act against agency plans, its position would usually triumph because the agencies did not have the resources or the statutory powers to prevail against resolute legislators.

Similarly, congressional committees found it easier to change agency action when they could prohibit the bureau from embarking on some course than when they required agencies to take specified positive steps. The Interior committees relied on the Bureau of Indian Affairs to develop plans for the termination of tribes, and the agency was able to slow action by procrastinating. Legislators frequently lamented their inability to goad the FDA into taking stronger action against suspected carcinogens. The frustration of legislators with congressional oversight probably stems from this negative bias. Although I have discussed the positive contributions of congressional oversight, committee staff members were usually not enthralled with oversight because they did not feel that it accomplished very much. Using oversight to effect change depends on agency compliance with congressional directives, and such conformity is sometimes difficult to obtain. Oversight can be a powerful mechanism to induce agency action if the agency is convinced of the existence of a problem and persuaded that legislators are truly concerned about the issue, but such responses do not automatically result from congressional complaints.

Although committees had a difficult time encouraging the agencies to take certain steps, they could force action when they wanted to do so. Deadlines, frequent hearings, and periodic regulations were devices the committees used to prompt a bureaucratic response. The House Ways and Means and the Senate Finance committees persistently used these techniques when guiding the implementation of programs administered by the Social and Rehabilitation Service. Rather than wait for the agency, the committees even wrote the regulations for the Social Services Grant Program. It could be cumbersome and time-consuming to use these devices, but the committees had the control mechanisms to ensure that agencies complied with legislative directions.

These findings have obvious significance for ways to strengthen the legislature in its efforts to control the bureaucracy. Committees could write enabling statutes in such a way that agencies were forced to respond. The use of timetables is the most apparent way to do this, but devices such as sunset legislation could pressure an agency to demonstrate that it was making progress. Committees could decide to formulate implementation plans themselves rather than delegate this task to an agency. In the 1960s the Interior committees would not have had to worry about the foot-dragging of the BIA if they had written the termination plans themselves. Of course, these kinds of positive efforts require additional work by congressional committees, a contribution that may not always be forthcoming. An easier way to provide for congressional power is to give legislators a tool, such as the legislative veto, to block agency action. However, these devices serve only as negative checks; they do not stimulate action.

Many devices could enhance the legislature's control over the bureaucracy. Yet it is worthwhile to contemplate whether or not we want stronger legislative control. Because legislators are elected and administrators are not, it is a natural tendency to conclude that greater political control of the bureaucracy is always desirable.[7] But before reaching this conclusion, one should consider the contributions to policy making made by the bureaucracy and whether or not stronger legislative control devices would squelch those contributions.

Implications for Governing

The implications for governing of the self-interest model and the subgovernment variant are overwhelmingly negative. They portray a system that is dominated by parochial interests, difficult to change, and closed to new challenges. However, the policy model and the findings of this research yield a more optimistic view of the policy-making process. The system is more open to change, facilitates discussions over central policy questions, and provides for leadership by elected officials. If anything, it is the bureaucracy that could be too weak. It lacks effective strategies to prompt legislative action, defend itself against criticisms, and prevent the weakening of overarching policy guidelines.

The assumption that decision makers pursue their narrow self-interests does not lead to a very positive view of their actions. Legislators preoccupied with reelection pay too much attention to constituents, ignoring broader policy effects and avoiding responsibility for decisions.[8] Bureaucrats trying to maximize their budgets sacrifice good public policy and neglect important policy consequences in their quest to protect and expand their budgets.

The subgovernment variant does not reassure us. A subgovernment is seen as a body that has managed to define an issue to benefit its participants, closing out alternative perspectives and isolating itself from larger political forces. In one of the most insistent attacks, Theodore Lowi argues that subsystems have led to interest-group liberalism, an approach to governing that is inherently conservative.[9] Interest-group liberalism hinders social change because it enfranchises existing interest groups but blocks the inclusion of new interests. The public is shut out of the decision-making process, and elected leaders lose political responsibility and authority. With the decline of elected leadership, the system responds to the demands of organized interests but not to those of the larger public.

The policy model and the findings of this study provide a number of more positive implications. First, the system depicted by this study is more open to policy change. Policy change occurs from the pushing and pulling of the legislators and bureaucrats as they advance their respective aims. The consensus of the self-interest model is a stable, contented consensus that is unlikely to lead to policy change. An issue is defined in the same way year after year, key decision makers present the same interests year after year, and the emerging policy is the same year after year. Policy change can occur, but only when outsiders grab control of the issue, redefining it or bringing new perspectives into the debate. The policy model presents a much more unstable consensus, and policy change emerges from this dynamic set of interactions. Conflict can develop at any time. New issues emerge as a result of elections, personnel changes, or decisions by key policy makers to shift their focus. Bureaus raise problems for the legislature to address because of judicial decisions, complaints from program beneficiaries, or a signal from a chief executive that he is looking for a new approach.

One source of policy change is the willingness of committee members to seek new policy directions. Because of their policy interests, many legislators search actively for new issues to debate as well as new solutions to old problems. Legislators realize that a subcommittee or committee can be a forum to explore an intriguing issue, an opportunity to cover new ground on a difficult problem, or the chance to hold forth on an ideological position. These legislative entrepreneurs are able to place an issue on an agenda because they often hold committee leadership positions.

Policy change can also stem from policy experts, individuals who drudge through the complex, confusing, and sometimes trivial details of a policy area. These legislators and administrators might not see themselves as creative entrepreneurs searching for innovative policy solutions. But as they sift through the vast amounts of information that constitute feedback, they uncover problems and labor to find workable solutions. The policy changes they generate may not be glamorous, startling, or dramatic, but they recognize bugs and kinks that "outsiders" would never see.

Policy change also occurs because subgovernments are not insulated from larger political forces. Participants in subgovernments are not immune to the forces that affect other political actors. Elections tell subgovernment members as well as outsiders about national moods and important issues. Interest groups will not ignore committee members, especially when the committee has jurisdiction over the issue of concern. For example, members of the Interior committees could not isolate themselves from anxiety about environmental degradation, especially when their committees wrote much of the protective legislation. In addition, subgovernment members may jump at the chance to address issues raised by outsiders. President Nixon's interest in Indian affairs brought forth a set of dramatic policy changes as key legislators and bureaucrats realized this was an opportunity for policy innovation. President Eisenhower's reluctance to have the government sell power shaped debates over reclamation even after he was president. Finally, outsiders can easily become insiders when personnel changes, in both agencies and committees, bring along new issues and perspectives. Membership changes on the Interior committees quickly brought eastern legislators into the debate over reclamation. Civil servants in the Bureau of Reclamation who "came of age" during the dustbowl days have slowly been replaced by administrators who grew up celebrating Earth Day.

Second, because the system is more open to policy change, it allows for broader policy representation. Government decision makers do not merely respond to organized groups; they also set agendas and structure debates according to their own interests. As they search for ways to advance their policy goals, decision makers are open to a wide variety of interests. Thus, policy areas will pick up the dominant debates, reflecting the overarching issues addressed by government decision makers. Because critical perspectives can find an audience, policy making is not isolated or removed from major issue concerns. This representation comes from the legislative committees and administrative agencies that make up a subgovernment as well as the political leaders—primarily the president—who are traditionally seen as standing outside the subgovernment.

We think of legislators as representing the views of their constituents introduced to them through elections, informal meetings with constituents, a sense of the district, and the activities of interest groups.[10] A typical criticism of Congress is that its members pay too much attention to constituents, ignoring the need for responsible governing.[11]

Members of Congress are often portrayed as individuals responding to the demands of interest groups and constituents, rather than individuals structuring and channeling those demands.[12] In fact, this view of interest groups and legislators lies behind the typology of the subgovernment variant. A main reason distributive policy is expected to be consensual is the belief that only the beneficiaries of the programs will be organized; those who pay the costs will not. Regulatory and redistributive policies become more conflictual because both of the opposing sides will be politically active.

In this study the legislators on the committees responded to interest-group demands, yet the congressional committees were not merely a point of access for vested interests. Several conflicts developed as legislators reacted to the complaints of interest groups adversely affected by a bureau's decision or inaction, but new interest groups were able to challenge the dominant interests. Environmental arguments were raised effectively in the 1960s before the full-fledged environmental movement began, and in the 1970s Interior Committee members responded quickly to the need for greater environmental protection.

Although interest groups are important sources of issues, seeing legislators as mere conduits for their positions results in an incomplete picture of the committees. Policy representation occurs when legislators decide to target issues for action in order to meet their own interests. It is not my intention to argue that every legislator on every committee has critical policy goals he or she wishes to advance. Clearly, we know from research on Congress that legislators juggle their goals, paying attention to one goal at one time and turning to another later on.[13] But for the representation of key policy issues it is not necessary to involve every legislator all of the time. This is why the preference outliers of the policy model are so important. An individual who decides to target an issue or specialize in a policy area can exert influence out of proportion to his or her numerical standing in the chamber. It only requires one legislator to bring an issue to the attention of the committee if he or she has the ability to set items on its agenda.

We are accustomed to thinking about representation by legislators, but the bureaucracy is also an important source of policy representation.[14] As it pushes forward with its views of appropriate and desirable public policy, it may advance policy views that are not picked up by legislators. This representation can be as straightforward as presenting the interests of a constituency. When an agency ties its mission to the interests of a particular group, it also forwards the concerns of that group, both directly and indirectly.

But the policy representation provided by the bureaucracy can be more complicated—and more important—than the representation of a particular group's interests. The bureaucracy may push the legislature to develop general principles and to ensure that past policies are consistent with those principles. In its quest for defensible public policies, the bureaucracy seeks overarching guidelines to direct its decisions. The legislature, on the other hand, may be more likely to grab onto case-by-case decision making as a relatively easy way to balance conflicting values and interests. An agency's opposition to this case-by-case law making, such as the FDA's concern with exemptions for specific drugs and food additives, may be one of the few forces pushing the legislature to develop general rules and principles.

A final contribution of the bureaucracy to policy representation is insights into implementation. Administrators will have a better idea of how long it may take to set up a new program, revamp standard operating procedures, or structure a program to meet judicial and executive requirements. Legislators, even if they follow an agency closely, will not have the same awareness of the possibilities and pitfalls of program implementation. Often administrators will point out that a certain approach cannot possibly succeed. This role as a naysayer can lead to criticisms of the bureaucracy, especially for its inertia, but an evaluation of the feasibility of a plan is crucial for its successful implementation. In addition, with a short time frame guided by the next election, legislators often want instant results, and the bureaucracy can remind them that a more steadfast and persistent effort may be necessary to accomplish programmatic goals.

A more open system allows for policy representation by political leaders officially outside of the subgovernment. The greatest concern, of course, is directed at the president, so often portrayed as helpless in the face of a strong subgovernment. But a more open system provides a president with the opportunity to define issues and present policy solutions, even in distributive policy areas. Eisenhower's election introduced a partisan and ideological issue into reclamation, and the issue was framed in those terms even after he was replaced by a Democratic president. By emphasizing fiscal conservatism, the Reagan Administration was able to reduce the role of the federal government in financing water projects.

Researchers have pointed at President Carter's highly visible failure to block water projects through his "hit list" as unequivocal evidence of the barriers to presidential influence in distributive policy.[15] But Carter's failure stemmed primarily from the strategy that was used to stop the projects. Unlike the Reagan Administration, which forwarded a general principle of fiscal conservatism that could then be picked up by legislators with similar views, the Carter Administration advanced a perspective that directly challenged Congress as an institution. Carter did not only argue that Congress had made lousy decisions in the past, he also challenged the authority of the institution to appropriate funds. Thus, his strategy alienated legislators who might have supported his position on its merits.

Some presidents will be successful at introducing new issues and policy solutions, yet others will fail, even in the same policy area. There is nothing inherent in the type of policy itself that determines the mode of decision making and thus the respective influence of various political actors. Rather, research on the president and Congress should focus on the dynamics of their interactions, questioning the use and success of various strategies.

Third, this more open and dynamic system with representation of diverse and changing policy views provides for greater leadership by elected officials. Key legislators, the preference outliers of the policy model, set agendas and structure debates. Legislators do not simply follow the interests of organized groups; their policy interests prompt them to respond to new interests and to seek out positions that may not be pushed by any one group. Presidents can alter the focus of debates by raising new issues and calling for innovative policy solutions. Although it will not always choose to use those control mechanisms, Congress has the resources to prevail in any battle with the bureaucracy.

The conclusion that we have a stronger legislature would seem inconsistent in light of the frequent complaint that the bureaucracy has excessive political power. According to this allegation, the bureaucracy, relying on its expertise and clientele support, can triumph over the legislature. Because it has little interest in developing any expertise and a high demand for the agency's programs, the legislature can be manipulated by a bureaucracy trying to maximize its budget. This may not be so troublesome if we believe the bureaucracy is led by altruistic, thoughtful administrators who only want to further the public interest.

But it is problematic if we believe the primary motivating force of the bureaucracy is the protection and expansion of its budget, especially when it faces a legislature with little inclination to guide or control bureaucratic behavior.

But a central conclusion of this research is not that a passive legislature is bested by an aggressive bureaucracy. To the contrary, it could be the bureaucracy, not the legislature, that is too weak. The legislature, through its careful scrutiny of administrative actions and its aggressive attacks on the agencies, undermines the legitimacy of the bureaus. In the face of these attacks, agencies have few strategies they can use to create political backing. They find themselves in a defensive posture, trying to fend off individual attacks but unable to generate enduring and deep-seated political support. With its legitimacy weakened and little support for its missions, the bureaucracy is then unable to contribute effectively to the policy-making process.

An aggressive legislature interested in controlling the bureaucracy will not undermine it automatically, but several characteristics of congressional intervention contribute to the weakening of the administrative agencies. Directions sent by Congress to an agency are often inconsistent, both over time and across committees, as legislators respond to changing economic conditions and varied societal goals and values. An agency that tries to respond to these conflicting directives in hopes of satisfying the legislature appears fickle and capricious; an agency that does not seems stubborn and willful, placing its priorities above those of elected officials. Also, legislators grant special exemptions from general rules to certain products or types of businesses. These exemptions challenge the principles that the bureaus are supposed to follow, suggesting that they are injudicious and unreasonable in general, not merely in the specific circumstances undergoing debate. Finally, legislators often have unrealistic expectations about the amount of time needed to implement a program and the likelihood that the program will have its intended effect. When agencies cannot meet these standards, they are easily portrayed as dilatory or incompetent. Even well-intentioned and thoughtful congressional intervention can lead to skepticism of an agency's motives, doubts about the bureau's ability to perform, or suspicions that the agency's actions are irrational.

These consequences of congressional intervention are magnified by the political environment of the American bureaucracy, an environment that recognizes the need for government intervention yet distrusts the intrusion into the lives of individuals and businesses. Thus, an agency always faces nagging beliefs that government intervention, by definition, is unnecessary, unwarranted, and undesirable. With little underlying support for agencies' programs, criticisms of the agencies reinforce questions about their legitimacy.

The notion that bureaus have little underlying support for their existence may seem inconsistent with the fact that few are actually eliminated. But many endure attacks on their programs designed to cut back or eliminate their responsibilities. Even more complain that they are established to accomplish a particular mission but then never given the resources to take effective action and constantly questioned when they do move. Thus, the mere existence of an agency does not demonstrate support for its mission.

If agencies had strategies to defend themselves successfully, we would not need to fret about challenges to the authority and legitimacy of the bureaucracy. Generally, we assume that an agency can build political support by manipulating program benefits.[16] When following this strategy, agencies can target benefits at legislators holding positions of influence if they need only a few votes to maintain their program. If they need to garner the endorsement of a number of legislators to save a controversial program, they can expand its size and scope. Because members of Congress want to "bring home the bacon" in hopes of getting reelected, this strategy is supposed to have high payoffs for the agencies.

This strategy may work when it can be used, but its usefulness is very limited. First, it requires program benefits that can be disaggregated. Some bureaus administer programs with grants or specific projects that can be separated in distinct parts, but others do not. These agencies cannot follow the strategy directly, although they could try to torque it around to meet their own needs. Unfortunately, this could very well lead to greater, not less, opposition because it would paint the agency as arbitrary, willful, and hypocritical. For example, to placate a protesting representative, a regulatory agency charged with protecting the public's interest could grant an exemption from a rule to a specific business located in that member's state or district. But this exemption would only anger those who believe the bureau panders to industry, leading to charges that the agency was violating the public's trust. An agency could try to appease these conflicting viewpoints by forging compromises, but then it could be charged as timid, irresolute, and unable to advance the interests it is charged with protecting. Thus, the agency, by trying to appease the opposition, only upsets its supporters.

Second, the strategy is not very effective during periods of scarce resources because it depends on the ability to expand a program. Lack of money due to budget deficits is one obvious constraint, but other resources needed to expand a program may be limited, too. For example, the Bureau of Reclamation had a difficult time building a coalition for the Colorado River Basin Project because there was not enough water to satisfy everyone's demands, not because they lacked the funds needed to construct a number of projects. Even when sufficient resources exist to satisfy everyone's demands, those requests could be contradictory, making it difficult to come up with solutions that would mollify all sides.

Without this strategy to pursue, an agency must resort to a discussion of the merits of its program. Yet that requires jumping into the thicket of the controversy because it was the merits of the program that were under attack in the first place. As we have seen, agencies are not very successful when they try to convince a disgruntled legislative committee that its complaints are unwarranted and that the perspective of the administrators is correct. This is especially the case when the agency is trying to persuade the committee members that legislative action is necessary.

The scenario of a weak bureaucracy may seem unduly alarming, but it is not unrealistic. Of the four agencies included in this study, the Bureau of Indian Affairs seemed to be especially weak. It was not considered an effective advocate for Indian tribes, especially when confronting more powerful agencies and interest groups. It accepted a circumscribed jurisdiction in the 1960s and 1970s. It was criticized for its ineptness by those who believed it should be stronger and more forceful. Although one could always argue that the administrators of the BIA were the problem, it is difficult not to believe that the constant attacks on the agency undermined its authority and vitality. The other agencies had not reached the weakened state of the BIA, but there were signs that they could. The Social and Rehabilitation Service was never able to pull together its disparate programs to create a vibrant agency assisting the disadvantaged. The Bureau of Reclamation's central mission has been all but eliminated, and it has not found other tasks to replace it. The Food and Drug Administration had to administer complex and confusing laws, such as the Delaney clause, while its implementation was undermined by special exemptions.

One might wonder whether a weak bureaucracy is actually a problem and not an advantage in a political system. With few independent sources of authority, a weak bureaucracy would be extremely pliant. Agencies would follow the directives of legislators and executives. Thus, in return for strengthening presidential and congressional controls over the administration, we would achieve greater responsiveness to elected officials. The dilemma in democratic theory created by an administrative state with a source of power independent of elected representatives would not arise.

Such a perspective, however, ignores the contribution the bureaucracy can make to policy making. We often establish an agency to be an advocate for a particular group. We expect agencies to know if a program is feasible, if it can be implemented successfully without deleterious effects. We expect agencies to administer general rules and principles without caving in to pressures for special treatment. We expect agencies to coordinate the diverse efforts of various organizations, as well as the different requirements of numerous programs. We expect agencies to push forward and address problems for which the legislature can find no solution. Without independent authority, agencies will not be able to perform these tasks effectively, and they will neither supplement nor balance the demands and interests of elected officials.

Conclusion

The Founders of the United States national government designed a structure that encouraged conflict, yet we are confused about the place of the bureaucracy in the institutional struggles that have ensued. This research has found that conflict between the bureaucracy and congressional committees is inevitable. The perspectives of bureaus and committees diverge because each body responds differently to various forces. As each institution pushes forward with its own views of what is necessary and desirable public policy, disputes between the two arise.

There is little reason to try to minimize these conflicts. They are rarely destructive. Conflict does not disrupt standard practices of decision making nor does it indicate that the bureaucracy is flagrantly abusing its power and running roughshod over the legislature. To the contrary, conflict between bureaus and committees is beneficial for policy making because each institution presses forward with its own views of desirable public policy, enriching subsequent decisions.

Even though democratic theory holds that the legislature should have the upper hand in this struggle, a bureaucracy clashing with the legislature need not be cause for concern. There is little reason to try to achieve greater legislative dominance. The legislature has the necessary control devices to prevail in any dispute with the bureaucracy. Enhancing this legislative control could be detrimental to the political system because the ability of the bureaucracy to contribute to policy making would be curtailed. The insights and perspectives of the bureaucracy are not always those of the legislature, but they are often important views that can shape and enrich public policy.

Notes

1. Herbert Kaufman, *Are Government Organizations Immortal?* p. 34.

2. Richard Cyert and James March, *A Behavioral Theory of the Firm*, pp. 120–122.

3. Joel Aberbach, *Keeping a Watchful Eye*, pp. 175–183.

4. Ibid., pp. 19–47.

5. Ibid., pp. 221–222.

6. For example, Morris S. Ogul, *Congress Oversees the Bureaucracy.*

7. For a discussion of a bureaucracy that is too weak relative to the power of elected officials, see B. Dan Wood, "Does Politics Make a Difference at the EEOC?" pp. 503–530.

8. Gary C. Jacobson, *The Politics of Congressional Elections*, pp. 211–223.

9. Theodore J. Lowi, "The Public Philosophy: Interest Group Liberalism," pp. 5–24.

10. Richard F. Fenno, Jr., *Homestyle: House Members in their Districts.*

11. Jacobson, *The Politics of Congressional Elections.*

12. James Q. Wilson, "The Politics of Regulation," in James Q. Wilson, *The Politics of Regulation*, pp. 357–394.

13. John Kingdon, *Congressmen's Voting Decisions.*

14. Frederick C. Mosher, *Democracy and the Public Service.*

15. Randall B. Ripley and Grace A. Franklin, *Congress, the Bureaucracy, and Public Policy*, p. 112.

16. R. Douglas Arnold, *Congress and the Bureaucracy*; and John A. Ferejohn, *Pork Barrel Politics.*

Appendix on Research Design

Qualitative analysis and case studies are two commonly used research approaches. Single and comparative case studies comprise some of the more common—and the more notable—research on both legislative and bureaucratic behavior. The case study approach, however, raises questions about the possibility of generalizing from a single case or even a number of selected cases and about the possibility of replicating the study.

Although we tend to believe that generalizing from quantitative analysis is more legitimate than generalizing from the results of a single case study, it is still possible to draw conclusions from a case study that can be applied to other settings. Lawrence Mohr, in an especially perceptive piece, shows that quantitative analysis is not prima facie better than a case study.[1] In an excellent book on case study research, Robert Yin argues that one can generalize from a single case study by producing conclusions that can be tested in other settings.[2]

The research design for this study was carefully considered in order to bolster the legitimacy of the findings and the possibility of generalizing those conclusions. The research design is a comparative and longitudinal case study. First, I selected the four agencies for theoretical reasons. As I explained in Chapter One, literature on subgovernments uses a typology to explain differences across policy areas. This study includes an agency from each of the policy areas forming the basis of the subgovernment variant. Second, the research design for this study is longitudinal. The twenty-four years of this study, 1961 to 1984, cover a period during which both Democrats, with positive views of government, and Republicans, skeptical of government intervention in the economy, controlled the presidency. Because the study is not cross-sectional, it is difficult to argue that a different time period would have produced different findings.

Case studies can be done using either qualitative or quantitative analysis. Quantitative analysis would not have been appropriate, nor would it have yielded many rich insights into the relationships between agencies and congressional committees. First, although it would be possible to count these conflicts in order to develop a quantitative measure of a dependent variable, such counting would have been arbitrary. Conflict is neither always well bounded nor delimited; it is not easy to determine when it develops and when it arises. Second, any counting mechanism tends to miss variations in degree and intensity. Qualitative analysis is more suited to a discussion of a fluid, changeable phenomenon.

This qualitative analysis rested on systematic, rigorous research and the use of multiple sources of data. The most difficult task was to reconstruct the legislative histories for the four agencies. To determine what interactions between the agencies and the committees actually occurred, I first read all of the germane articles in the *Congressional Quarterly Almanac* and the *National Journal* and any books or articles on the policy area that I could find. Because I recognized that these documents might not tell the whole story, I then interviewed relevant personnel. I began the interviews by asking the respondents what issues they considered important and then used their replies throughout the rest of the interview. When additional information was needed to clarify and verify points, I turned to congressional hearings, committee reports, and the Congressional Information Service (CIS) abstracts.

Information collected through the interviews was critical. Respondents were used as informants and spoke about both agencies and committees. Although the interviews were unstructured, I asked certain types of questions to all respondents. The questions focused on what issues were critical, what positions were advanced by the agencies and the legislators, and how differences on the issues were resolved. I also asked the individuals to verify information I had collected from other sources.

Fifty individuals were interviewed during 1984 and 1985. The average length of the interviews was sixty-five minutes; the shortest interview was twenty minutes, and the longest was 140 minutes. I spoke with three members of Congress, seventeen congressional staff members, twenty-nine bureaucrats, and one White House assistant. Individuals were selected by the positions they held, and I also asked them to recommend other persons who would be helpful. Most of the agency officials held top positions in the various divisions of the bureaus, and I located them by using the Yellow Pages of the Federal Directory. Only one person refused to speak with me; one suggested I talk to his superior, which I did. Several members of Congress agreed to meet with me, but we were unable to arrange appropriate times for any appointments.

Archival material for this time frame was not yet in the National Archives but was stored in the Federal Records Center. I asked to see legislative files; permission to use the material had to be granted by the agency. Archival material was used for the Bureau of Indian Affairs and the Bureau of Reclamation. Permission was not granted by officials from the Food and Drug Administration or the Social and Rehabilitation Service.

Notes

1. Lawrence Mohr, "The Reliability of the Case Study as a Source of Information," pp. 65–94.

2. Robert K. Yin, *Case Study Research: Design and Methods.*

Bibliography

Aberbach, Joel. *Keeping a Watchful Eye*. Washington, DC: The Brookings Institution, 1990.

Aberbach, Joel, Robert Putnam, and Bert Rockman. *Bureaucrats and Politicians in Western Democracies*. Cambridge: Harvard University Press, 1981.

Appleby, Paul. *Morality and Administration in Democratic Government*. Baton Rouge, LA: Louisiana State University Press, 1952.

Arnold, R. Douglas. *Congress and the Bureaucracy*. New Haven: Yale University Press, 1979.

Bendor, Jonathan, and Terry M. Moe. "An Adaptive Model of Bureaucratic Politics." *American Political Science Review* 79 (September 1985), pp. 755–774.

Berkman, Richard L., and W. Kip Viscusi. *Damming the West*. New York: Grossman Publishers, 1973.

Bernstein, Marver. *Regulating Business by Independent Commission*. Princeton: Princeton University Press, 1955.

Bullock, Charles S., III. "U.S. Senate Committee Assignments, Preferences, Motivations, and Success." *American Journal of Political Science* 29 (November 1985), pp. 789–808.

Butler, Raymond. "The Bureau of Indian Affairs: Activities since 1945." *The Annals of the American Academy of Political and Social Science* 436 (March 1978), pp. 50–60.

Califano, Joseph A., Jr. *Governing America*. New York: Simon and Schuster, 1981.

Cater, Douglass. *Power in Washington*. New York: Random House, 1964.

Chubb, John E. *Interest Groups and the Bureaucracy: The Politics of Energy*. Stanford: Stanford University Press, 1983.

Clausen, Aage. *How Congressmen Decide: A Policy Focus*. New York: St. Martin's Press, 1973.

Cohen, Michael, James March, and Johann Olsen. "A Garbage Can Model of Organizational Choice." *Administrative Science Quarterly* 17 (March 1972), pp. 1–25.

Cohen, Warren, and Philip Mause. "The Indian: The Forgotten American." *Harvard Law Review* 81 (June 1968), pp. 1818–1858.

CIS Annual Abstracts. Washington, DC: Congressional Information Service, 1971 to 1984.

Congress and the Nation. Washington, DC: Congressional Quarterly Service. vol. 1–6 (1945–1984)

Congressional Record. 1961 to 1985.

Congressional Quarterly Almanac. Washington, DC: Congressional Quarterly Service, 1960 to 1985.

Congressional Quarterly Weekly Reports. Washington, DC: Congressional Quarterly Service, 1960 to 1985.

Cyert, Richard, and James March. *A Behavioral Theory of the Firm*. Englewood Cliffs, NJ: Prentice Hall, 1963.

Davidson, Roger H. "Subcommittee Government: New Channels for Policy Making." In *The New Congress*, ed. Thomas Mann and Norman Ornstein, pp. 99–133. Washington, DC: American Enterprise Insitute, 1981.

Davidson, Roger H., and Walter J. Oleszek. *Congress and Its Members*. Washington, DC: Congressional Quarterly Press, 1985.

Davies, J. Clarence, and Barbara S. Davies. *The Politics of Pollution*. Indianapolis: Bobbs-Merrill, 1975.

DeLoria, Vine, Jr. *Behind the Trail of Broken Treaties*. New York: Delacorte Press, 1974.

———. *Custer Died for Your Sins: An Indian Manifesto*. New York: Macmillan, 1969.

Derthick, Martha. *Uncontrollable Spending in Social Service Grants*. Washington, DC: The Brookings Institution, 1975.

Dodd, Lawrence C., and Richard L. Schott. *Congress and the Administrative State*. New York: Wiley and Sons, 1979.

Downs, Anthony. *Inside Bureaucracy*. Boston: Little Brown, 1967.

Edelman, Murray. *The Symbolic Uses of Politics*. Urbana: University of Illinois Press, 1964.

Eisner, Marc Allen, and Kenneth J. Meier. "Presidential Control versus Bureaucratic Power: Explaining the Reagan Revolution in Antitrust." *American Journal of Political Science* 34 (February 1990), pp. 269–287.

The Environmental Defense Fund and Robert H. Boyle. *Malignant Neglect*. New York: Alfred A. Knopf, 1979.

Fenno, Richard F., Jr. *Congressmen in Committees*. Boston: Little, Brown, 1973.

———. *Homestyle: House Members in their Districts*. Boston: Little, Brown, 1978.

Ferejohn, John A. *Pork Barrel Politics*. Stanford: Stanford University Press, 1974.

Fisher, Louis. "Judicial Misjudgments about the Lawmaking Process: The Legislative Veto Case." *Public Administration Review* 45 (Special Issue, November 1985), pp. 705–711.

———. "One Year after *INS* v. *Chadha*: Congressional and Judicial Developments." Washington, DC: Congressional Research Service, 1984.

Fiorina, Morris P. *Congress: The Keystone of the Washington Establishment*. New Haven: Yale University Press, 1977.

Forbes, Jack D. *Native Americans and Nixon: Presidential Politics and Minority Self-Determination 1969–1972*. Los Angeles: University of California, 1981.

Frank, Jerome. *Courts on Trial: Myth and Reality in American Justice.* Princeton: Princeton University Press, 1949.

Freeman, J. Leiper. *The Political Process: Executive Bureau-Legislative Committee Relations.* New York: Random House, 1965.

Fritschler, A. Lee. *Smoking and Politics: Policymaking and the Federal Bureaucracy.* Englewood Cliffs, NJ: Prentice-Hall, 1983.

Gais, Thomas L., Mark A. Peterson, and Jack Walker. "Interest Groups, Iron Triangles and Representative Institutions in American National Government." *British Journal of Political Science* 14 (April 1984), pp. 161–185.

Grenzke, Janet Miller. *Influence, Change, and the Legislative Process.* Westport, CT: Greenwood Press, 1982.

Havender, William R. "The Science and Politics of Cyclamates." *The Public Interest* 71 (Spring 1983), pp. 17–32.

Hayes, Michael. *Lobbyists and Legislators: A Theory of Political Markets.* New Brunswick: Rutgers University Press, 1981.

Heady, Bruce. "A Typology of Ministers: Implications for Minister–Civil Servant Relationships in Britain." In *The Mandarins of Western Europe,* ed. Mattei Dogan, pp. 63–86. New York: Wiley and Sons, 1975.

Heclo, Hugh. *A Government of Strangers.* Washington, DC: Brookings, 1977.

———. "Issue Networks and the Executive Establishment." In *The New American Political System,* ed. Anthony King, pp. 87–124. Washington, DC: The American Enterprise Institute, 1978.

Holden, Matthew. "Imperialism in Bureaucracy." *American Political Science Review* 60 (December 1966), pp. 943–951.

Jacobson, Gary C. *The Politics of Congressional Elections.* Boston: Little, Brown, 1987.

James, Dorothy Buckton. *The Contemporary Presidency.* New York: Bobbs-Merrill, 1974.

Janssen, William. "FDA since 1938: The Major Trends and Developments." *Journal of Public Law* 13 (1964), pp. 205–221.

Jones, Charles O. *Clean Air: The Policies and Politics of Pollution Control.* Pittsburgh: University of Pittsburgh Press, 1975.

———. *The United States Congress.* Homewood, IL: Dorsey Press, 1982.

Kammer, Jerry. *The Second Long Walk: The Navajo–Hopi Land Dispute.* Albuquerque: University of New Mexico Press, 1980.

Kanter, Rosabeth Moss. *Men and Women of the Corporation.* New York: Basic Books, 1977.

Kaufman, Herbert. *Are Government Organizations Immortal?* Washington, DC: The Brookings Institution, 1976.

———. *The Forest Ranger: A Study in Administrative Behavior.* Baltimore: Johns Hopkins Press, 1960.

Keiser, K. Robert. "The New Regulation of Health and Safety." *Political Science Quarterly* 95 (Fall 1980), pp. 479–491.

King, Anthony. "Ideas, Institutions and the Policies of Governments: A Comparative Analysis." *British Journal of Political Science* 3 (July and October 1973), pp. 291–313, 409–423.

Kingdon, John. *Agendas, Alternatives, and Public Policies.* Boston: Little Brown, 1984.

————. *Congressmen's Voting Decisions*. 3d ed. New York: Harper and Row, 1989.

Kvasnicka, Robert M., and Herman J. Viola, eds. *The Commissioners of Indian Affairs 1824–1977*. Lincoln: University of Nebraska Press, 1979.

Levitan, Sar A., and Barbara Hetrick. *Big Brother's Indian Programs—With Reservations*. New York: McGraw-Hill, 1971.

Lipsky, Michael. "Protest as a Political Resource." *American Political Science Review* 60 (December 1966), pp. 1144–1158.

Lowi, Theodore J. "American Business and Public Policy, Case Studies and Political Theory." *World Politics* 16 (July 1964), pp. 677–695.

————. *The End of Liberalism: The Second Republic of the United States*. New York: Norton, 1979.

————. "The Public Philosophy: Interest Group Liberalism." *American Political Science Review* 61 (March 1967), pp. 5–24.

Maass, Arthur. *Congress and the Common Good*. New York: Basic Books, 1983.

————. *Muddy Waters: The Army Engineers and the Nation's Rivers*. New York: Da Capo, 1974 (c. 1951).

Madison, James. *The Federalist Papers*.

Malbin, Michael J. *Unelected Representatives*. New York: Basic Books, 1980.

Mann, Dean. "Political Incentives in U.S. Water Policy: Relationships Between Distributive and Regulatory Politics." In *What Government Does*, ed. Matthew Holden, Jr., and Dennis L. Dresang, pp. 94–123. Beverly Hills: Sage, 1975.

Masters, Nicholas. "Committee Assignments in the House of Representatives." *American Political Science Review* 49 (June 1955), pp. 345–357.

Mayhew, David. *Congress: The Electoral Connection*. New Haven: Yale University Press, 1974.

McCool, Daniel. "Subgovernments and the Impact of Policy Fragmentation and Accommodation." *Policy Studies Review* 8 (Winter 1989), pp. 264–287.

Meier, Kenneth J. *Politics and the Bureaucracy*. Monterey, CA: Brooks/Cole, 1987.

Melnick, R. Shep. *Regulation and the Courts*. Washington, DC: Brookings, 1983.

Miles, Rufus, Jr. "The Origin and Meaning of Miles' Law." *Public Administration Review* 38 (September/October 1978), pp. 399–403.

Mills, Gregory, and John Palmer, eds. *Federal Budget Policy in the 1980s*. Washington, DC: The Urban Institute, 1984.

Mintz, Morton. *By Prescription Only*. Boston: Houghton Mifflin, 1967.

Mohr, Lawrence. "The Concept of Organizational Goal." *American Political Science Review* 67 (June 1973), pp. 470–481.

————. "The Reliability of the Case Study as a Source of Information." In *Advances in Information Processing in Organizations*, ed. Lee S. Sproull and Patrick Larkey, vol. 2, pp. 65–94. Greenwich, CT: JAI Press, 1985.

Morrow, William L. *Congressional Committees*. New York: Charles Scribner's Sons, 1969.

Mosher, Frederick C. *Democracy and the Public Service*. New York: Oxford University Press, 1982.

Moynihan, Daniel Patrick. *Maximum Feasible Misunderstanding*. New York: Free Press, 1969.

Muckleston, Keith W. "Water Projects and Recreation Benefits." In *Congress and the Environment*, ed. Richard A. Cooley and Geoffrey Wandesforde-Smith, pp. 112–129. Seattle: University of Washington Press, 1970.

Nadel, Mark V. *The Politics of Consumer Protection.* New York: Bobbs-Merrill, 1971.

Nash, Roderick. *Wilderness and the American Mind.* New Haven: Yale University Press, 1982.

The *National Journal.* Washington, DC: Government Research Corp. 1969 to 1985.

The National Wildlife Federation. *Shortchanging the Treasury.* May 22, 1984.

The *New York Times.* 1960 to 1985.

Niskanen, William. "Bureaucrats and Politicians." *Journal of Law and Economics* 18 (December 1975), pp. 617–644.

————. *Bureaucracy and Representative Government.* Chicago: Aldine, 1975.

Officer, James E. "The Bureau of Indian Affairs since 1945: An Assessment." In *The Annals of the American Academy of Political Science* 436 (March 1978), pp. 61–71.

Ogul, Morris S. *Congress Oversees the Bureaucracy.* Pittsburgh: University of Pittsburgh Press, 1976.

Olson, Mancur. *The Logic of Collective Action.* Cambridge: Harvard University Press, 1971.

Peltzman, Sam. "Toward a More General Theory of Regulation." *Journal of Law and Economics* 19 (August 1976), pp. 211–240.

Pertschuk, Michael. *Revolt Against Regulation.* Berkeley: University of California Press, 1982.

Price, David E. *The Commerce Committees.* New York: Grossman Publishers, 1975.

Pringle, Lawrence. *Water: The Next Great Resource Battle.* New York: Macmillan, 1982.

Quirk, Paul J. *Industry Influence in Federal Regulatory Agencies.* Princeton: Princeton University Press, 1981.

Randall, Ronald. "Presidential Power versus Bureaucratic Intransigence: The Influence of the Nixon Administration on Welfare Policy." *American Political Science Review* 73 (September 1979), pp. 795–810.

Redford, Emmette S. *Democracy in the Administrative State.* New York: Oxford University Press, 1969.

Reinhold, Robert. "Pills and the Process of Government." In *Federal Administrative Agencies*, ed. Howard Ball, pp. 157–162. Englewood Cliffs, NJ: Prentice-Hall, 1984.

Rhodes, Susan L. "Political Conflict and Technological Uncertainty in Bureaucratic Policy Making: The Food and Drug Administration's Regulation of Intrauterine Devices." Presented at the Annual Meeting of the Midwest Political Science Association, 1982.

Ripley, Randall B., and Grace A. Franklin. *Congress, the Bureaucracy, and Public Policy.* Homewood, IL: Dorsey Press, 1984.

Robinson, Michael C. *Water for the West: The Bureau of Reclamation, 1902–1977.* Chicago: Public Works Historical Society, 1979.

Rohde, David, and Kenneth Shepsle. "Democratic Committee Assignments in the

House of Representatives: Strategic Aspects of a Social Choice Process." *American Political Science Review* 67 (September 1973), pp. 889–905.

Rosenbaum, Walter. *The Politics of Environmental Concern.* New York: Praeger, 1973.

Rosenbloom, David. "Accountability in the Administrative State." In *Accountability in Urban Society*, ed. Scott Greer, Ronald Hedlund, and James L. Gibson, pp. 87–114. Beverly Hills: Sage, 1978.

Sabatier, Paul A. "An Advocacy Coalition Framework of Policy Change and the Role of Policy-Oriented Learning Therein." *Policy Sciences* 21 (1988), pp. 151–157.

————. "Knowledge, Policy-Oriented Learning, and Policy Change: An Advocacy Coalition Framework." *Knowledge: Creation, Diffusion, Utilization* 8 (June 1987), pp. 649–692.

Salisbury, Robert H. "The Analysis of Public Policy: A Search for Theories and Roles." In *Political Science and Public Policy*, ed. Austin Ranney, pp. 151–175. Chicago: Markham, 1968.

Scher, Seymour. "Conditions for Legislative Control." *Journal of Politics* 25 (August 1963), pp. 526–551.

Seidman, Harold. *Politics, Position, and Power.* New York: Oxford University Press, 1980.

Selznick, Philip. *TVA and the Grassroots.* Berkeley, CA: University of California Press, 1949.

Shepsle, Kenneth, and Barry Weingast. "Legislative Politics and Budget Outcomes." In *Federal Budget Policy in the 1980s*, ed. Gregory Mills and John Palmer, pp. 343–384. Washington, DC: The Urban Institute, 1984.

Smith, Jane F., and Robert M. Kvasnicka, eds. *Indian–White Relations: A Persistent Paradox.* Washington, DC: Howard University Press, 1981.

Smith, Steven, and Christopher Deering. *Committees in Congress.* Washington, DC: Congressional Quarterly Press, 1984.

Sorkin, Alan. *American Indians and Federal Aid.* Washington, DC: The Brookings Institution, 1971.

Stevens, Robert, and Rosemary Stevens. *Welfare Medicine in America.* New York: The Free Press, 1974.

Stigler, George. "The Theory of Economic Regulation." *Bell Journal of Economics and Management Science* 2 (Spring 1971), pp. 3–20.

Sundquist, James. *The Decline and Resurgence of Congress.* Washington, DC: The Brookings Institution, 1981.

————. *Politics and Policy: The Eisenhower, Kennedy, and Johnson Years.* Washington, DC: The Brookings Institution, 1968.

Taylor, Serge. *Making Bureaucracies Think.* Stanford: Stanford University Press, 1984.

Taylor, Theodore W. *American Indian Policy.* Mt. Airy, MD: Lomond Publications, 1983.

Turner, James. *The Chemical Feast.* New York: Grossman Publishers, 1970.

U.S. Congress. House. Committee on Education and Labor. H Report 92–282. 92d Cong., 1st sess., 1971.

————. House. Committee on Education and Labor. H Report 93–244. 93rd Cong., 1st sess., 1973.

————. House. Committee on Education and Labor. Select Subcommittee on Education. *Hearings to Amend the Older Americans Act of 1965.* 93rd Cong., 1st sess., 1973.

————. House. Committee on Education and Labor. Select Subcommittee on Education. *Oversight Hearings on Older Americans.* 93rd Cong., 1st sess., 1973.

————. House. Committee on Government Operations. *Hearings on Drug Safety, Part 1.* 88th Cong., 2d sess., 1964.

————. House. Committee on Interstate and Foreign Commerce. Subcommittee on Oversight and Investigations. *Medical Devices Regulation: The FDA's Neglected Child.* 98th Cong., 1st sess., 1983.

————. House. Committee on Interstate and Foreign Commerce. Subcommittee on Public Health and the Environment. *Hearings on FDA Oversight—Food Inspection.* 92nd Cong., 1st sess., 1971.

————. House. Committee on Interstate and Foreign Commerce. Subcommittee on Public Health and the Environment. *Hearings on Food Labelling and Food Inspection.* 92nd Cong., 2d sess., 1972.

————. House. Committee on Interstate and Foreign Commerce. Subcommittee on Public Health and Welfare. *Hearings on FDA Consumer Protection Activities—FDA Reorganization.* 91st Cong., 1st and 2d sess., 1969–1970.

————. House. Committee on the Interior. Subcommittee on Indian Affairs. *Hearings on Indian Resource Development Act of 1967.* 90th Cong., 1st sess., 1967.

————. House. Committee on the Interior. Subcommittee on Indian Affairs. *Hearings on Policies, Programs, and Activities of the Department of the Interior.* 87th Cong., 1st sess., 1961.

————. House. Committee on the Interior. Subcommittee on Indian Affairs. *Hearings on Policies, Programs, and Activities of the Department of the Interior.* 88th Cong., 1st sess., 1963.

————. House. Committee on the Interior. Subcommittee on Indian Affairs. *Hearings on the Establishment of the American Indian Policy Review Commission.* 93rd Cong., 2d sess., 1974.

————. House. Committee on the Interior. Subcommittee on Irrigation and Reclamation. *Hearings on the Burns Creek Project.* 87th Cong., 1st sess., 1961.

————. House. Committee on the Interior. Subcommittee on Irrigation and Reclamation. *Hearings on the San Felipe Division of the Central Valley Project, California.* 90th Cong., 1st sess., 1967.

————. House. Committee on Ways and Means. Subcommittee on Oversight. *Hearings on AFDC Quality Control Program.* 94th Cong., 1st sess., 1975.

————. House. Committee on Ways and Means. Subcommittee on Oversight. *Hearings on HEW Efforts to Reduce Errors in Welfare Programs.* 94th Cong., 2d sess., 1976.

————. Senate. Committee on Finance. *Hearings on Medicare and Medicaid.* 91st Cong., 1st sess., 1969.

————. Senate. Committee on Finance. S Report 93–249. 93rd Cong., 1st sess., 1973.

————. Senate. Committee on Labor and Public Welfare. S Report 93–1139. 93rd Cong., 2d sess., 1974.

————. Senate. Committee on Labor and Public Welfare. Subcommittee on Health. *Hearings on Cosmetic Safety Act of 1974.* 93rd Cong., 2d sess., 1974.

————. Senate. Committee on Labor and Public Welfare. Subcommittee on the Handicapped. *Hearings.* 92nd Cong., 2d sess., 1972.

————. Senate. Committee on the Interior. *Hearings on the Realignment of the BIA Central Office.* 93rd Cong., 1st sess., 1973.

————. Senate. Select Committee on Indian Affairs. *Hearings on Closing of Off-Reservation Boarding Schools.* 97th Cong., 2d sess., 1982.

————. Senate. Select Committee on Indian Affairs. *Hearings to Amend the Native American Programs Act of 1974.* 98th Cong., 2d sess., 1984.

————. Senate. Select Committee on Indian Affairs. *Oversight Hearings on Indian Education.* 97th Cong., 2d sess., 1982.

Walker, Jack. "Setting the Agenda in the U.S. Senate: A Theory of Problem Selection." *British Journal of Political Science* 71 (October 1977), pp. 423–445.

Warne, William E. *The Bureau of Reclamation.* New York: Praeger, 1973.

Warwick, Donald. *A Theory of Public Bureaucracy.* Cambridge: Harvard University Press, 1975.

Weingast, Barry R., and Mark J. Moran. "Bureaucratic Discretion or Congressional Control? Regulatory Policymaking by the Federal Trade Commission." *Journal of Political Economy* 91 (October 1983), pp. 765–800.

Wheeler, William Bruce, and Michael McDonald. *TVA and the Tellico Dam.* Knoxville: University of Tennessee Press, 1986.

Wildavsky, Aaron. *The Politics of the Budgetary Process.* Boston: Little Brown, 1983.

Wilson, James Q. *The Investigators: Managing FBI and Narcotics Agents.* New York: Basic Books, 1978.

————, ed. *The Politics of Regulation.* New York: Basic Books, 1980.

Wilson, Woodrow. "The Study of Administration." *Political Science Quarterly* 2 (1887), pp. 197–222.

Wood, B. Dan. "Does Politics Make a Difference at the EEOC?" *American Journal of Political Science* 34 (May 1990), pp. 503–530.

Yaffee, Stewart Lewis. *Prohibitive Policy: Implementing the Federal Endangered Species Act.* Cambridge: MIT Press, 1982.

Yin, Robert K. *Case Study Research: Design and Methods.* Beverly Hills, CA: Sage, 1984.

Index

About the Author

Cathy Marie Johnson is a professor of political science at Williams College. She has written articles on the behavior of new agencies, gender and bureaucracy, and state policies toward sin.